Violence in Today's School Workplace:

Protecting Teachers and School Employees in a Violent Age

---

*Your Guidebook for Coping with
Today's School Violence, and Understanding
Three of the Major Forces Involved
in this Nationwide Crisis*

Diane H. Williamson, Ed. D.
Child Psychologist

David E. Strecker, Attorney
Labor Law Attorney

Henry D. Townsend, C.S.P.
Safety and Health Consultant

K&M Publishers, Inc.
Tulsa, Oklahoma, USA
www.kmpublishers.com

Copyright © 2007 by
K & M Publishers, Inc.
Post Office Box 701083
Tulsa, OK 74170-1083, USA

ISBN: 0-9727134-6-8

All rights reserved. Printed in the United States of America.
This publication is protected by copyright.

Written permission must first be obtained from the Publisher prior to any prohibited reproduction, storage in a retrieval system, or transmission in any form or by any means: electronic, mechanical, photocopying, recording, or likewise.

Important Note

Products and services provided by K&M Publishers, Inc., are intended for educational purposes only. K&M Publishers, Inc., makes no warranties or guarantees, either expressed or implied, as to the legal effect of the information supplied in those products and services. Further, K&M Publishers, Inc., assumes no liability associated with providing this information. You are encouraged to seek the advice of your own legal counsel or that of your sponsoring agency or entity regarding this material. For information about permission(s), write to:
> Rights and Permissions Department
> K&M Publishers, Inc.

Production work by
Enfield Lowhill Publisher Services
Tulsa, Oklahoma
(www.enfieldlowhill.com)

Cover design by
Welch Design
Tulsa, Oklahoma

Photography by
BW Studios
Tulsa, Oklahoma

To order, or for more information:
www.kmpublishers.com

About The Authors

Dr. Diane H. Williamson earned her Bachelor's and Master's degrees from the University of Tulsa, and holds a Doctor of Education from Oklahoma State University. She completed postdoctoral training at the University of Oklahoma College of Medicine; Forest Institute of Psychology; the Menninger Clinic; New England Medical Center; and the Neurological Center in Dallas. Her major areas of professional training include human development and neuro-psychology. Her professional interests include human development and the effects of brain functions on learning and behavior. Dr. Williamson is a member of the American Psychological Association, and a board member of the Tulsa Chapter of the National Association for Mental Illness. Dr. Williamson has worked as a special education teacher and consultant for Tulsa Public Schools. She taught at the University of Wisconsin-Eau Claire and at Langston University in Tulsa. She also consults with hospitals and social service agencies in the Tulsa area.

Dr. Williamson is deeply committed to the challenge presented by today's disturbed youth – both in a pressure-packed school or domestic environment. Her involvement in – and resolution of – thousands of such cases qualifies her as an extraordinary author. She provides both a causal background as to the progression of these disturbed personalities, and what steps are necessary to prevent them, or at least be more alert to their danger signs.

David E. Strecker, J.D., M.I.L.R. is the 1995 founder and Managing Partner of Strecker & Associates, P.C., Tulsa, Oklahoma. Mr. Strecker has over 30 years experience in the litigation field. Strecker & Associates' exclusive practice in labor and employment law has given the firm wide recognition and praise in Oklahoma and neighboring states. It is known as one of the most sophisticated, substantial employment law practices in the entire region. He received his Law Degree (cum laude) and Masters of Industrial Labor Relations Degree from Cornell University. He holds a B.A. Degree (magna cum laude) from Westminster College in Missouri. David was a Lt. Colonel in the U.S. Army Judge Advocate General's Corps.

He teaches Labor Relations at Oklahoma State University. He is a member of the Oklahoma and New York State Bar, as well as the U.S. Supreme Court. He is admitted to practice before several federal courts in Oklahoma, Arkansas, New York and Texas. David is former General

Counsel and Vice President of the Tulsa Area Human Resource Association. He brings a wealth of hands-on experience in the many legal matters surrounding the escalation of violence and the related litigation in our schools. He is well suited to add his expertise in legal and labor relations litigation to this book.

Henry D. Townsend, C.S.P. is President of *LosStop Consultant's, Inc.*, Tulsa, Oklahoma, specialists in Loss Control and Environmental Compliance. Henry has over 36 years of experience in the development, implementation and administration of Safety, Health and Environmental Compliance Programs. This includes work in the relatively unrecognized area of Bloodborne Protection requirements for people not employed in the medical care industry. A graduate of the University of Miami in Coral Gables, with a Bachelor of Business Administration degree, he also served in Merchant Marine Safety in the U.S. Coast Guard.

His global and domestic employment both as a corporate safety director and a consultant includes the U.S. Government, college instructor, petrochemical and medical electronics manufacturing, petroleum industry/manufacturing, heavy metal fabrication plants, and food processing sites. Mr. Townsend is a Professional Member of the American Society of Safety Engineers (ASSE) and a full member of the American Industrial Hygiene Association (AIHA), as well as being a Certified Safety Professional for 16 years. He currently serves as Chairperson of the Tulsa County Local Emergency Planning Committee.

Acknowledgments

The Authors and the Publisher wish to acknowledge and thank those who contributed to the writing of this book – those who encouraged our writing, typed our manuscript, read our material, and continually reminded us that such a book is very much needed.

Further we are indebted to the many state, local and federal agencies that so generously allowed us to research their material and include some of it in this book.

It is our hope this team effort will result in attaining the goal for writing this book: A Call To Action! A change agent that shows school workplace employees – from classroom teacher to school bus driver to the cafeteria worker – that violence against you (and between students) *is not* the norm. That there is absolutely no justification for anyone to be abused or violated by anyone else. That there is help available to all injured parties.

But even more important, is that there are means of stopping this vicious, endless cycle of increasing school violence. We offer you our support, our insight, and we wish you every success establishing your own school non-violence programs.

Good Luck!

Diane H. Williamson, *Ed.D., Child Psychologist*

David E. Strecker, *Labor Law Attorney*

Henry D. Townsend, *C.S.P., Safety/Health Consultant*

By Way of ... Introduction

This book is the unique, proactive viewpoint of three professionals who are gravely concerned about the devastating, deep wound effects of violence and bloodshed in our modern school workplace.

These highly skilled practitioners, each from their field of expertise, pour into this book their combined decades of hands-on experience in three main forces involved in this disruptive trauma our dedicated educators and staff must grapple with daily. *Isn't their focus supposed to be just to educate, mature, and enlighten our children?*

But now, three overarching, non-education concerns have crashed the school house and shoved education aside:

1. *The legal rights, concerns and recourse for all parties involved with violence;*
2. *Aberrant student behavior and how to manage it;* and
3. *Health-Safety protection.*

This team-writing approach to this festering problem eliminates your need to research data in the three professions comprising this book and areas of school violence. Instead, these distinguished authors piece together a string of proactive logic and solutions to this perplexing issue our educators and staff face. An honest effort has been made to provide a useful collection of references and resources for the proactive amongst you who want to research, explore and take action now to slay this growing monster.

Of course, no single source can provide an easy, comprehensive solution to the open-ended problems making up this boiling cauldron. You are strongly advised to talk with school administration and/or your attorney before finalizing any solutions to resolve this challenge.

We are confident this book breaks new ground, giving every one of you confidence and motivation, and opening many eyes to this complex set of issues our school workers live with. This is not a cookbook containing ready, easy solutions. It is more to let you know that, while yes, there is a problem, you are not facing it alone – there are sources of support and justice.

Let there be no doubt – these veterans from three diverse fields have worked hard to make this book flow logically and be useful. We welcome you to their writings.

The Publisher

Table of Contents

About the Authors v
Acknowledgments vii
Introduction viii

Part I. A LEGAL PREFACE
David E. Strecker, Labor and Employment Law Attorney

1. INTRODUCTION TO THE LAW AND LEGAL TERMS 3
   The Structure of the Law: The Nature of Law and Its Sources

2. THE LAW PERTAINING TO SCHOOL VIOLENCE AND ITS 13
   PREVENTION
   The Duty to Protect Against Violence: "In the Good Old Days"

3. LEGAL TOOLS TO PROTECT OTHERS AND OURSELVES 29
   FROM VIOLENT ACTS
   – Limits on Student Discipline and Self-Defense
   – Status of Corporal Punishment in the Fifty States 50
   as of July 2006.

Part II. THE ROLE OF CHILD DEVELOPMENT, BEHAVIOR AND LEARNING IN THE PREVENTION OF SCHOOL VIOLENCE
Dr. Diane H. Williamson, Ed.D., Child Psychologist

4. DEVELOPMENT PRINCIPLES: INFANCY, EARLY 57
   CHILDHOOD, AND ADOLESCENCE

5. THE DEVELOPMENTAL STAGES 63

6. EFFECTIVE MANAGEMENT OF SCHOOL VIOLENCE 87
   PREVENTION
   – Behavior Management

Part III. BLOODBORNE PATHOGENS (BBP), AND RELATED SAFETY ISSUES
Henry Townsend, CSP, Safety & Health Consultant

7. DISEASES CONTRACTED FROM BBP AND REQUIRED 99
   PROACTIVE MEASURES

8. REGULATORY PROTECTION AGAINST BBP DISEASES   113
   FOR SCHOOL WORKPLACE EMPLOYEES

9. THE APPLICATION OF THE OSHA BBP STANDARD   139
   AND THE PUBLIC SCHOLASTIC WORKPLACE

APPENDICES

Appendix A – U.S. Department of Labor Directory of   161
    States with Approved Occupational Safety and
    Health Plans

Appendix B – Sample Workplace Violence Policy Statement   166
    (Sample Format)

Glossary of Terms   167

PART I

A Legal Preface

Oliver Wendell Holmes was a famous 19th Century lawyer, judge and legal scholar. He was ultimately appointed to the United States Supreme Court. But he did not live in an ivory tower. A veteran of the Civil War, he was wounded in combat and schooled in the hard realities of war. Long after that experience he summed-up the true nature of law.

He said: "The life of the law has not been logic: it has been experience." Holmes knew that the law was not some academic exercise, but developed in response to the needs of society and as a reaction of society to our experience (including our mistakes).

As you read this book you need to keep Holmes' statement in mind. No single book can make you a legal expert or even acquaint you with all the laws you need to know. What I will attempt to do here in Part I is give you a legal (and practical) framework to use when you think about, or encounter problems at your workplace whether in the classroom, on a school bus, in the corridor, or on the playground.

The best legal advice I can give you can be summed-up in a simple phrase: *Use your common sense and experience when making decisions.* As Justice Holmes implied, much of the law is based on common sense and experience - not the experience of lawyers or judges - but the experiences of the average person in our society.

So you should not feel intimidated when you hear or read about huge jury verdicts against school districts or school employees. These things will always be possible in our society. Sometimes the verdicts are mistakes, made by juries. More often, however, they involve school employees doing exactly the opposite of what common sense would have told them to do. They often involve school officials reacting to a situation out of anger or frustration. They sometimes involve a person taking action for personal reasons, rather than basing their actions on what would be best for the school and its students. Finally, they are occasionally due to a school employee who has not been properly trained in performing their duties.

If you read and remember the topics discussed in these Legal Issues chapters, it will give you added confidence to deal with difficult people and situations that you encounter at work. There is nothing magical or mysterious about the law. Fortunately, it is not like learning how to speak a foreign language or attempting to master a strange type of mathematics. The basics are easy to learn. Perhaps you know some of them already!

Chapter One

An Introduction to the Law and Legal Terms

THE STRUCTURE OF THE LAW

The Nature of Law and its Sources

There are some special laws governing schools and we will get to these shortly. Before we do, however, it is important to understand that, in the eyes of the law, a school, a school bus, a playground, an athletic field, or other school settings are usually subject to all of the laws and rules that apply to other institutions of our society.

A *Law* is a rule or set of rules that govern our behavior. There are usually penalties for violating a law - these are sometimes referred to as the *"Teeth of the Law."* There are two basic places where we go to find laws: Statutes and Court Decisions.

Statutes are laws enacted by a legislative body. This could be the Congress of the United States or your own state legislature. This might also include the laws enacted by the governing body of a city or town, such as a city council. Instead of being called "Statutes" however, such laws are usually referred to as *Ordinances*.

Court Decisions. Laws can also be created by courts. This is known as ***Common Law*** or ***Judge Made Law.*** Sometimes courts create law when there is not statute covering the area. At other times, courts interpret vague or unclear provisions of statutes, and such interpretations become a part of the law. It is difficult to summarize Common Law, because one has to read many court cases to get the *"Big Picture."* One of the things this book will do is summarize the Common Law as it applies to the issue of violence in the school setting.

Constitutions are found at both the federal and state level. Constitutions are a type of statute because a legislative body of some sort usually creates them. Of course, we all learned in school how the U.S. Constitution came into being as the result of the efforts of our Founding Fathers. States also have constitutions usually created by the state legislature, special conventions, or territorial legislatures at about the time the state was admitted to the union. Constitutions are different from normal legislation in two respects.

First, they are usually more basic than legislation in that they deal with such issues as the fundamental rights of citizens, the structure of government, and the electoral process. Second, they are more difficult to amend or repeal than a normal statute. Usually, to amend a constitution it takes more than a majority vote of the legislature, or perhaps even a vote of the people (or the states).

In modern times, some laws create ***Administrative Agencies*** to enforce them. An example of this would be the *Equal Employment Opportunity Commission* created by Congress to enforce the Civil Rights Act of 1964. Some administrative agencies may be created by a state legislature to enforce laws it enacts. An example of this might be a state agency created to enforce a state's environmental laws.

The ***Regulations*** created by an administrative agency are not strictly law but often have the force of law. In other words, we had better follow them unless we can show that the agency went beyond what it was supposed to do – that is, it exceeded the power given to it by the legislative body that created it. For our purposes, however, if your school district is governed by rules created by an agency, such rules should be followed. It is important to know that courts ordinarily will give great weight to an agency's rules and its interpretation of those rules.

Civil and Criminal Law

The law can also be looked at in at least two other ways. First is whether the law is Civil or Criminal. ***Civil Law*** pertains to rules which, if broken, the violators are "punished" by (1) monetary penalties often referred to as ***Damages***, and (2) orders of a court to comply with the law in the future (these orders known as ***Injunctions***). ***Criminal Law*** also lays down rules. If these rules are broken, however, the wrongdoer is subject to imprisonment as well as monetary penalties – often called ***Fines.***

Some laws are both civil and criminal. A good example of this would be federal laws dealing with securities fraud. Someone who breaks these rules could be liable to be sued in civil court or prosecuted in criminal court (or both), depending on which rule or rules he or she broke.

Civil Law

Civil Law is usually enforced through lawsuits. These lawsuits are filed by individuals or companies (or organizations) against the person or company they claim violated their rights. Trials are often conducted in front of a jury who will make a decision once all the evidence has been presented to them. Sometimes a jury verdict does not have to be unanimous, depending upon the state involved and the size of the jury. The person bringing the lawsuit is known as the ***Plaintiff.*** The person defending is the ***Defendant.*** The Plaintiff has the burden of proof. In other words, he or she must prove the case by a *"preponderance of the evidence."* This means that the Plaintiff must show their claims are more than likely true. If the evidence is evenly balanced, the Plaintiff loses because he or she has failed to carry the burden of proof.

Criminal Law

Criminal Law is enforced through law enforcement personnel (police, etc.) and through the district attorney, county prosecutor or similar official. Criminal trials are often conducted with a jury. The government has the burden of proof to prove guilt *"beyond a reasonable doubt."* The jury verdict must usually be unanimous. This burden of proof is much higher than the "preponderance of evidence" standard used in civil trials.

When Laws Conflict

We can also look at the law as a "pecking order". Because of the ***Supremacy Clause*** in the U.S. Constitution, federal law will always be at the top of the pecking order. In other words, if a federal law and a state law conflict, the federal law will control. For instance, some state laws say women are not allowed to work in certain occupations. Federal law, however, says women can work in *any* occupation. In this instance, federal law "trumps" state law. It works the same way if a state law and city ordinance conflict. The state law will always control.

Also, a constitution will always win over a statute or a court decision. You have probably heard of a court decision that holds a law to be "unconstitutional". This means the court decided that there was a conflict between the constitution and the law. If a law is in conflict with a constitution, the constitution always trumps (wins).

Chapter 1 - Structure of the Law

The Judicial System

Court systems differ widely from state to state. Some generalities hold true, however, in almost all states. One of these is that there is a "pecking order" in the judicial system. The ***Trial Court*** is the lowest court in the pecking order of courts. This is the court that conducts the jury trial whether it is civil or criminal. Some states have separate criminal courts, but most states provide for only one court system to try both civil and criminal cases at the Trial Court level.

Next is the ***Intermediate Appellate Court,*** sometimes called the *Court of Appeals.* It hears cases that are appealed by the losing party at the Trial Court level. The party not liking the decision of this court may appeal it to the highest state court, usually called the ***State Supreme Court.*** Further appeal is usually not available unless federal issues are raised allowing an appeal into the federal system.

Appellate courts do not usually hear witnesses or hold hearings where evidence is introduced. They decide cases on a "paper record" of what happened in the Trial Court, and on the basis of *Briefs* submitted by the parties. A *Brief* is a written argument as to why a party should win the appeal. Sometimes an Appellate Court will allow the parties to present an oral argument in front of the court, in addition to submitting Briefs.

In the federal system, the upward pecking order is as follows: ***United States District Court, Circuit Court of Appeals,*** and the ***United States Supreme Court.*** A United States District Court will have jurisdiction over cases that arise in a geographical area known as the ***District.*** An example would be the United States District Court for the Northern District of New York. Courts of Appeals are organized around a geographic area known as a ***Circuit.*** The Circuit is usually comprised of all the district courts in a group of several states. An example of this would be the United States Court of Appeals for the Tenth Circuit, which includes the district courts in the states of Utah, Oklahoma, Colorado, Kansas, New Mexico, Wyoming and Montana.

Some states have special appeals courts to hear particular kinds of cases. For instance, some states have an Appellate Court dealing only with criminal cases. Other states have a special court dealing with appeals in the Workers Compensation System.

The Fundamentals of Tort Law

A **Tort** is defined as *a wrong done to another person*. Beyond this, a Tort is *a wrong for which the law will provide a remedy*. A tort is a civil wrong, and not criminal in nature. Some torts may also be crimes. For instance, assault is both a civil wrong and a criminal violation in most states. Other torts, such as negligence, are usually civil only. Torts may be either *Intentional Torts* or *Negligence-based Torts*.

Intentional Torts

Intentional Torts include assault, battery, causing another person severe emotional distress, conversion (taking another's property), slander, libel or false imprisonment. The key element here is that the actor intends to commit the act in question. He or she may not intend the precise harm caused by the act, but nevertheless will be liable for all harm caused.

For instance: I become angry with a co-worker and hit him, thinking only to teach him a lesson for insulting me. My blow is harder than I thought it would be. His skull is fractured and he is disabled for life. Even though I did not intend to cause such severe harm, I will be liable for the harm done because I did intend to commit the tort of battery.

An *Assault* is an act that puts another person in reasonable fear of bodily harm. If I come at you with a baseball bat and start to swing it, I have assaulted you. If I throw a stapler at you and miss, I still have committed an assault. *Battery* is *an unlawful act of physical touching.* A blow, a push, a shove, hitting someone with an object – are all considered batteries.

False Imprisonment consists of an unjustifiable confinement of another person, either literally (as in locking them in a room), or through threats of harm to them or to others (example: telling someone they cannot leave a room until they have confessed to a crime).

In some cases, the law allows us to do harm to another person. *Self-Defense* or *Defense of Another* are the two main examples of this. If you reasonably fear that someone is about to do harm to you or to another person, you are allowed to use whatever force is necessary to prevent the harm. In most states, deadly force may only be used — if necessary — in self-defense (or defense of another) to prevent death or serious bodily injury. In some states, if you can remove yourself from danger, you must attempt to do this before defending yourself. This is known as the **Duty to Retreat.** Other states do not recognize this principle, but only require that you reasonably perceive you are in danger of being harmed. In those states, you may defend yourself even if you could retreat.

Negligence

Before you can be sued for a tort based on negligence, there must be a *Duty* on your part either to act or refrain from acting. If you have no duty, then you cannot be liable. For instance: assume I am walking down the street and see two strangers fighting each other. It appears one is gaining the advantage and is about to seriously injure the other. I do nothing and the person is seriously injured.

Am I liable because I should have done something to stop the violence? The answer? **No.** You may say that I had a moral obligation to stop the violence and you might be correct. But I had no *legal* obligation to break up the fight, because I had no duty under the law to do so.

If however, you do have a duty to another person, then you must act reasonably, and can be held liable for any harm done to that person caused by your negligence. "When does one person owe a duty to another?" A good example is a parent's duty to his or her child. Another example: a duty owed by those who operate public transportation (such as a bus driver) to their passengers. School personnel may also have a duty to protect students, and the school system may also owe a duty to its employees. We will discuss these important issues later in these chapters.

Negligence can consist of either taking action or a failure to act. If I drive my car at night without my lights on and have a wreck because no one can see me, I have committed a *Negligent Act.* I will be liable for any harm this act causes to others. If I am the driver of a bus and notice a passenger having what appears to be a heart attack and I do nothing, I have failed to act in a situation where I had a duty to act. Once again, this is considered to be negligence, and I may be liable to the passenger.

For me to be liable to pay damages, the negligence must be the *Proximate Cause* of the harm. In other words, my negligent act must have directly led to the damage. If I cause a car accident by running into the rear of another car, I am certainly liable for the damage to the other car, and to those injured in the crash. But if the driver of the car I hit is wanted by the police, and he runs away from the scene and is struck by another car, I am not liable for his injuries because they were not directly caused by my negligence.

Proximate Cause is often measured in terms of what would be the reasonably foreseeable results of the negligence. In other words, I know that if I drive my car negligently, it could cause harm to other cars or people as the result of a crash. But if some harm happens that is not a natural or probable result of my negligence, then this harm is not proximately caused by my negligence. In the previous example given, I could not have reasonably foreseen that the driver of the other car would commit such a rash act as running out into traffic.

Sometimes, the duties we have are imposed by statutes or regulations, and not by common law doctrines. We will discuss many of these statutes as they pertain to schools in later chapters.

Chapter Two

The Law Pertaining to School Violence and its Prevention

THE DUTY TO PROTECT AGAINST VIOLENCE

"In The Good Old Days"

Many states have laws that give immunity to school districts and their employees, at least under certain circumstances. These laws mostly still exist, but their scope of protection has been weakened. In the past there was also a feeling that the law should not be concerned about bullies and the like. *After all, wasn't this just a part of growing up?*

There was much resistance to converting teachers and administrators into law enforcement personnel or policemen. This was not their job. Beyond this, it was felt that parents had the primary obligation to control children. The schools were there to reinforce parental discipline, but were not thought of as the primary source of behavioral control.

Indeed, in the past, schools were not breeding grounds for serious violence except on very rare occasions. At worst, what "violence" existed was viewed as playground roughhousing. If anything, schools were viewed as safe havens in an increasingly dangerous world.

Unfortunately, as with many other things in our society, the good old days are gone. In fact, they were probably gone before the 1999 Columbine Incident in Colorado. They were certainly gone after that tragic incident occurred and grabbed the attention of our horror-struck country. It forced us to realize that serious violence can happen. The shocker? Even in relatively affluent school settings! This incident (and many others that happened afterwards) has us scrambling for answers to numerous questions.

The *Good Old Days* also were given a serious blow by the United States Supreme Court in 1999. In a case involving sexual harassment (as opposed to traditional violence), the Court held that school districts <u>could be</u> liable for **student vs. student** sexual harassment under Title IX of the Education Amendment of 1972 if the district or its employees were "deliberately indifferent to ... severe, pervasive, and objectively offensive" harassment.[1] The message of this case is that schools cannot sit idly by in the case of violence or harassment which has risen to the level of being serious and/or frequent.

In many states, the immunity of school districts has been eroded by statutes and court decisions. For instance, school employees may lose their immunity if they are grossly negligent. In other situations, teachers may have immunity for their acts only for "on-the-spot" decisions which are not directly contrary to school policies.

The advent of "anti-bullying" legislation in many states, moreover, has underscored the need to rethink our attitudes about the role of teachers and administrators in the area of violence prevention.

The Reality

It is only realistic to put school violence in its proper perspective. The increased violence in our schools mirrors that in our entire society. No matter how much we try to prevent it, it is inevitable there will be some violence in both our society and therefore, in our schools. This is important to note because the legal duty of school districts and school employees *will not be able to absolutely insure against violence, but to do everything which is reasonably possible to prevent it and to deal with it effectively when it occurs.* What are the legal rights and obligations of teachers, administrators, and other school employees to deal with violence and protect students and others? These questions will each be addressed in the following pages.

THE DUTY TO PROTECT AGAINST VIOLENCE

General Principles

Believe it or not, in most states there is no affirmative duty on the part of school districts to be absolute insurers of student safety. A claim of failure to provide adequate security will usually fail. Compulsory school attendance laws simply do not create this duty under most state constitutions. ***This does not mean, however, that there is no duty to protect in certain circumstances.*** Compulsory attendance laws present in most states create a special relationship between the student and the school system – the kids are required to be at school. This results in increased responsibility on the part of teachers, school administrators and employees which other entities in our society — a retail store, for example — would not have. No one is required to go into a retail store but children have no choice about whether to be at school.

In some states, the law places school officials in a status known as *"in loco parentis."* Translated literally, it means *"in the place of the parents."*

In these states, the law says that the school official stands in the place of the child's parent and thus is required to use the same degree of care to protect the child as would the child's own parent. Parents, in sending their children to school, lose some of their power to protect the children. Thus, the duty belongs to the school officials who act in the place of parents. This is an old legal doctrine which has been around for over two hundred years.

In other states, statutes define the duty to protect students. Sometimes the statutes are general in nature and other times they speak to specific situations (such as school bus safety).

How can one cut through all of these statutes, judicial decisions, and constitutional provisions and give some practical advice which will be universally applicable? The bottom line is this: *when the risk of harm is reasonably foreseeable, the school district is under an obligation to take steps to prevent the harm and/or warn of the harm.*

It is important to note, however, in these situations the school officials must have been indifferent to the danger or acted in willful disregard for the student's safety.[2] For instance, if there have been incidents of bullying or violence on a bus, the school district can reasonably foresee that harm may result if something is not done to remedy the situation. If it wholly fails to do anything, it may be liable if a student is subsequently hurt. An important part of this doctrine is that acts of violence that "come out of the blue" with no warning by students who had no history of misbehavior will not normally result in liability for the school district or any school official.

Beyond this, it is almost universally accepted that the actions the school must take in response to foreseeable harm are only required to be reasonable, and are not required to rise to the level of a one hundred percent guarantee of security. Going back to the violence on the bus example, suppose that the school suspends or expels the offenders. These culprits then show up at the bus stop one day and commit an act of violence against the students waiting to board the bus. Most courts would hold that the school will not be liable for this because it did what was reasonable under the circumstances.

This "new bus violence incident" however, might give rise to a duty on the part of the school to take additional measures – such as alerting local law enforcement and requesting they be present at the bus stop.

Another way a duty to protect can arise is if a responsible school official gives specific assurances to a specific person or persons that they will be protected from danger and the person justifiably relies on this assertion. Thereafter, the official fails to do what they said they would do, then this directly results in harm to the person to whom the promise was made. For example, the school's star basketball player comes to an assistant principal complaining that he has been threatened with harm if he attends a basketball game that evening. The assistant principal assures the player that she will alert the appropriate security officials to protect him at the game.

The official forgets to do this; the player comes to the game, and is the victim of violence. This may well give rise to a valid claim against the school district. *Do not give assurances you cannot keep.* If what is being asked is beyond your power to provide, seek assistance.

Protection: The Duty to Supervise or Discipline Students

Related to the overall duty to protect students is the duty to supervise and discipline students. Failure to perform this duty could be (and often is) viewed as a failure to adequately protect students. Schools are under a duty to adequately supervise the students in their charge, and they will be held liable for *foreseeable* injuries *proximately caused* by the absence of adequate supervision. For the school or its officals to be liable under this doctrine, it must be shown that school authorities had sufficiently specific knowledge of the dangerous conduct that caused the injury. Further, the plaintiff must show that the chain of events that followed the negligent failure to supervise was a normal or foreseeable consequence of the situation created by the school's negligence.[3] Whether the student responsible had a prior history of similar violent conduct is very important in analyzing questions of liability under this rule. Usually there will be no liability to school or teacher for random acts of violence. In one case, a student was struck in the eye by a pencil thrown in the classroom by another student. The perpetrator had no history of misbehavior of this sort and, therefore, the act could not have been foreseen. No liability was found in this situation.[4] If, on the other hand, the student had been throwing things in class before and nothing was done to discipline the student, then liability might arise based on a failure to adequately supervise and discipline the student. This would be especially true if his antics had resulted in injury to someone else before.

Another case involved an assistant principal who failed to remove a student from a hallway after the student had been attacked. The student was thereafter attacked by a fellow student who was not involved in the prior attack. **The court held that there was no evidence that the assistant principal** *reasonably should have foreseen that the unknown assailant would sneak up behind the student and attack him.* The court ruled in favor of the school district.[5] Thus, even if negligence has occurred, there must be a direct relationship between the negligence and the harm. If, in this case, the person who had assaulted the student in the first place came back to renew his attack, the assistant principal's failure to remove the student from the hallway might have resulted in liability to the school district. *The reason for this is that it could be reasonably foreseen that the original attacker might renew the assault if given the opportunity. Leaving the student in the hallway put him in increased danger that this would happen.*

Once again, courts do not require that schools be insurers of student safety (although many teachers would say that it "seems that way" sometimes). In fact, court decisions take into account that schools have limited resources, and that sometimes judgment calls must be made to accommodate for personnel shortages and the like. As long as a school does what is reasonable with the resources it has, it should not be liable merely because an act of violence might have been prevented if they could afford more teachers or better security devices.

For instance, in one case a student was struck in the face during lunch on the playground. The teacher assigned to supervise this area was at lunch and the principal was patrolling another part of school grounds. The school was held exempt from liability because it acted within the proper discretionary function in determining the type of supervision which was required.[6] In fact, schools are afforded a great deal of discretion in determining what security measures are needed. This is particularly true when there has not been a track record of violence.

If, on the other hand, there have been numerous incidents of violence, the school will be required to do what it can within its resources to prevent future episodes. Willful indifference to this risk could well result in liability. To summarize, in this common law duty to supervise we see the following elements:

a. It comes into play while on school premises or at a school-sponsored activity.

b. It looks to the degree of certainty that an injury will occur if nothing is done to prevent it.

c. Whether there has been a prior occurrence of similar events is a very important factor in the analysis.

d. If the school would have taken some action to prevent the violence, the likelihood is that such action would have successfully prevented the violent episode in question.

The Duty to Warn

Sometimes the duty to protect is mainly a duty to warn or report. For instance, if you hear two students talking about injuring a third student, you may have an obligation not only to deal with the two students in question, but also you (or the school) may have an obligation to warn the potential victim or his or her parents about the threat.

What if it's "just a joke?" How do you distinguish between a joke and a real threat? There is no easy answer to this. Some of the factors the courts have looked at include: (1) the manner in which the threat was spoken; (2) the context of the conversation; (3) prior history of confrontation between the student and the potential victim; (4) past history of troubled behavior on the part of the person uttering the threat; and (5) your own knowledge of the speaker and his or her characteristics. It is *always* best to err on the side of safety. When it comes to threats, they have no place in schools, even as a joke. The bottom line is that you cannot just say to yourself, "It's none of my business" or wait until "I'm sure it's serious."

Also, you do not need to warn a group any larger than necessary to protect the person in question. Warnings would not be required in the case of young children who are not mature enough to take reasonable steps to protect themselves. In such cases, the parents should receive the warnings as well as others at school who may be in a position to protect the child; e.g., bus drivers, cafeteria workers, crossing guards and the like.

In many states, the school may be under a duty to report to law enforcement threats which are both credible and have the potential to result in imminent harm.

Statutory Approaches

Various state and federal statutes also impact the school's duty to protect students from violence.

A Word About Immunity

The statutes of some states (and in some cases Judge Made Law) give school districts immunity from most state law negligence claims. These laws differ greatly from state to state. Some states have very strong immunity laws affording substantial protection to the school and its employees. Texas is an example of this.

Individual employees of the school district may also be protected under these immunity laws if they are acting within the scope of their duties. Several states provide that immunity attaches when the act in question is discretionary, or involves an exercise of judgment as opposed to acts which involve no discretion (such as where rules control a teacher's conduct and there is no room to deviate). For instance, many "on the spot" decisions that do not specifically violate school policy might be protected by the immunity doctrines of many states.

Put another way, a school official may be entitled to immunity so long as his or her actions, *viewed from the perspective of the official at the time of the act*, can be said to be within the range of reasonableness. [7] Other states will deny immunity to a school employee who has engaged in "willful or wanton misconduct."

Even in states that have immunity statutes, however, courts have held that a school district may be liable if it can be shown that the district failed to protect a student from foreseeable harm. Furthermore, a state law immunity statute cannot shield the school district from liability under a federal law such as the ones discussed next.

Private schools and their employees usually do not enjoy immunity, at least in the same sense that public sector employees do. On the other hand, such schools and employees may not be liable under laws which only apply to governmental entities.

42 U.S.C. Section 1983

We will refer to this law as **Section 1983**. It is a federal law passed shortly after the Civil War and prohibits governmental entities (such as a school district) from depriving individuals of their constitutional rights.

It is one of the more frequently used federal statutes involved in suing school districts and their officials. Under this law, it has been held that although the state has no constitutional duty to protect its citizens from private violence, there are two exceptions to the general rule. The first is known as the "Special Relationship" Doctrine and the second is known as the "Danger Creation" Doctrine. The rule and exceptions are often traced to a United States Supreme Court case decided in 1989: *DeShaney v.Winnebago County Department of Social Services.* [8]

Under the special relationship doctrine, because the state has such extensive control over a person's life, a heightened duty arises to protect that person. This theory is often used in the case of prison inmates where the state has almost total control over the person involved. Most courts which have addressed the issue have held that mandated school attendance laws do not entail so restrictive a custodial relationship as to impose upon the school district the same duty as the state has to protect inmates at a prison. [9]

Thus, similar to the common law doctrine discussed earlier, there is no overarching duty to protect against violence under Section 1983.

It is possible, however, for a school district and its officials to be liable under the state-created danger exception to the general rule. This involves situations where the school district creates a *special danger*. It is not enough to show that the state merely increased the danger of harm from a third person. The plaintiff must also show that the school district acted with the requisite degree of culpability in failing to protect the plaintiff. Under the state-created danger theory, common elements found by the courts can be summarized as follows:

- The harm ultimately caused was foreseeable and fairly direct;

- The state official acted in willful disregard for the plaintiff's safety;

- There existed a relationship between state and plaintiff (a student's relationship with the school would satisfy this element); and

- The school used (or failed to use) their authority, resulting in the creation of an opportunity that otherwise would not have existed for the third party's crime to occur.[10]

In some instances, a failure to train teachers and school employees to deal with violence, when there has been a history of school violent acts, can run afoul of the state-created danger doctrine. In one case, the court found a principal liable under Section 1983 because, after a series of sexual assaults on a severely disabled child, he did nothing to train his subordinates to prevent such future assaults, and failed to implement any type of policy to prevent such assaults in the future. [11]

In general, the plaintiff must show that the school created or worsened the dangerous condition which ultimately caused the student's injury. It is also important the school knew of the risk, or that the risk was obvious and the school acted recklessly in conscious disregard of the risk.

In one of the cases stemming from the tragic shootings at Columbine High School in 1999, the court held that a successful claim under Section 1983 must prove there was either (1) an intent to harm someone, or (2) knowingly placing a person unreasonably at risk of harm. This court elaborated on the second "method." The court gave as an example where the public official was aware of a known or obvious risk which was so great that it was highly probable serious harm would follow, and he or she unreasonably and consciously disregarded the consequences. [12]

Gun Free School Act of 1994 [13]

This federal law applies to all schools which are receiving federal funding under the Elementary and Secondary Education Act. The law requires that any student found with a weapon on school grounds must be expelled for at least one year. Failure to do so can result in loss of federal funds under the Elementary and Secondary Education Act. This federal statute has resulted in many state legislatures passing what are known as "zero tolerance policies" which are discussed later. This law was repealed in 2002, but its provisions were incorporated in the *No Child Left Behind Act*.

No Child Left Behind Act [14]

This federal law was enacted in 2001 and has numerous, complicated provisions. Most of these provisions contain requirements which school districts must meet in order to receive federal funding.

A central provision of the law is found in Section 6736, entitled "Limitation on Liability for Teachers." Under this law, no teacher in a school shall be liable for harm caused by an act (or failure to act) of the teacher on behalf of the school if (1) the teacher was acting within the scope of the teacher's employment or responsibilities to the school; (2) the actions of the teacher were in accordance with Federal, State, and local laws in the furtherance of efforts to control, discipline, expel, or suspend a student or maintain order and control in the classroom or school; (3) the teacher was properly licensed, certified, or authorized by appropriate authorities for the activities involved; (4) the harm was not caused by willful or criminal misconduct, gross negligence, reckless misconduct or a conscious, flagrant indifference to the rights or safety of the individual harmed; and (5) the harm was not caused by the teacher operating a motor vehicle.

The law provides that if a state requires a mandatory training of teachers in risk management as a condition of limited liability, such laws are not impacted by the No Child Left Behind Act.

The law also contains limits on awards of **Punitive Damages** against teachers. Punitive damages are *those awarded to punish or make an example of someone whose conduct is deemed to be outrageous, wanton, or reckless*. Punitive damages can amount to hundreds of thousands of dollars and, in some cases, even more. Many of the large verdicts you may have read about in the papers involved an award of punitive damages.

The law provides that punitive damages may not be awarded against a teacher so long as the act was within the scope of the teacher's authority or employment. In order to get a punitive damage award against a teacher, the person suing must show by *clear and convincing evidence*, that the act of the teacher amounted to willful or criminal misconduct or a conscious, flagrant indifference to the rights or safety of the individual harmed.

There are some situations where teachers do not enjoy the limits on liability or punitive damages under this law. For instance, if the teacher's act constitutes a crime of violence, protection will not be afforded. The same holds true if the teacher's act constitutes a sexual offense, a violation of federal or state civil rights laws, or was committed under the influence of any intoxicating alcohol or drug.

The law does not affect any state or local law or policy pertaining to the use of corporal punishment.

Basically, what all this means is that teachers will have some limited protection if they act within their authority; do not violate any rule of law or policy, and act in good faith in an attempt to prevent violence or to enforce discipline at school. This protection is not one hundred percent, but it is better than none at all.

Significantly, the Act requires school districts to have policy requiring that any student who brings a firearm to school be referred to the criminal justice or juvenile delinquency authorities. [15]

The No Child Left Behind Act has other provisions which impact the area of school violence. For instance, the law requires that schools implement a school-wide program for potential educational problems. One element of this program must be a section dedicated to violence prevention.[16] Another section of the law describes the "principles of effectiveness" for combating violence and drugs in public schools. Such measures include gathering statistical data, scientific research, involvement of family and community members, etc.[17]

Anti-Bullying Legislation

Many states have passed laws known informally as "anti-bullying" legislation. These laws will vary from state-to-state. Some are more stringent than others, but all touch upon the duty of the school district to protect students against violent acts.

One common element of almost all of these laws is to require bullying education and to establish the duty of the school to report incidents of bullying to the state. Bullying is defined differently in these statutes, and often the statutes are not just directed against violent acts but also what may be characterized as harassment.

Zero-Tolerance Policies

Zero-Tolerance Policies are another way that legislatures have sought to protect students through the passage of statutes. Several states have enacted such policies which are usually enforced at the local school board level.

Although these policies will differ, a common element is the immediate suspension or expulsion of students who possess weapons on school grounds. These policies sometimes provide for alternative educational opportunities for offenders expelled under their terms. In some cases, it is left up to the school boards to determine what, if any, alternative education is available for the expelled student.

Some people have criticized these policies because of the harshness inherent in them, and also because the expelled student is often taken out of the educational system altogether. Many have suggested that this is counter-productive.

Summary of the Duty to Protect

What seems clear from reading all the statutes and case law on this subject is this: *a school owes a duty to its students and its employees to protect them from foreseeable harm.* Once the harm is foreseen, reasonable steps must be taken to render protection.

Common sense must be our guide. The law does not require the school official to have a crystal ball to predict the future. The law does not require you to take steps which would have no reasonable chance of preventing the violence. The law does not hold you to be a strict insurer against violence, especially random or unforeseen acts. The law does not require you to be a superman or superwoman, *but to only do what is reasonable and within your power to protect and/or warn.*

On the other hand, the law does not allow you to blind yourself to the warning signs of violence. It does not allow you to turn a deaf ear to pleas for help or threats. It does not allow you to ignore a history of violence or threats of violence when you are confronted with a situation.

The law is more lenient when you must make an "on the spot" decision than when you have the luxury of time to plan what you should do and consult with others about an appropriate course of action.

The bottom line is that, in the old days – where teachers could say that we're in the school business; we're **not** policemen or prison guards – are over. Now we will be judged, but judged by the standards of reasonableness and not by the rules of perfection or hindsight. In all cases, it is usually better to act than ignore.

Chapter Three

Legal Tools to Protect Others and Ourselves from Violent Acts

LIMITS ON STUDENT DISCIPLINE AND SELF-DEFENSE

In Chapter Two, we learned about our duty to protect students and others from violence and harm. We learned about the limitations on that duty. This Chapter Three will focus on some of the tools the law provides us with to discharge that duty. We also will discuss the limitations the law puts on these tools. Remember: because this book is written for a general school workplace audience, *always consult your local school policies (if any) on this and all other issues.*

Self-Defense and the Defense of Others

All states allow for a person to defend themselves, and also to defend others. Most state laws allow the use of force or violence in these situations - to some extent. If you reasonably perceive that you are about to be injured, you have the right to defend yourself, even to the extent of using force.

Naturally, you cannot use more force than is needed to prevent the offense.

This same right extends to the defense of others. If you reasonably perceive that someone else is in danger of harm, you have the same right to use whatever force is necessary (but no more than is necessary) to prevent the offense. It is often said that you go to someone else's defense at your peril because you have no more right to defend that person than he or she has to defend himself or herself. For instance: you see two people, A and B, fighting and you believe that A is the aggressor so you go to the aid of B. If it turns out that B was the aggressor, you might be liable for assault and battery. Of course, in the context of school settings, you have an obligation to prevent fighting and would have the right to put a stop to the fight.

Some other rules regarding self-defense are nearly universal. For instance, verbal insults and name calling, no matter how aggravating and contemptible, do not constitute justification for an assault. In other words, name calling does not justify a physical response. Second, the right of self-defense cannot be invoked by the aggressor or by one who voluntarily enters into difficulty with another. Third, even if a person is the aggressor in a fight, if he or she has withdrawn from the fray and indicates his or her desire for peace, your right of self-defense is ended. Simply put, if the aggressor backs off, you can't continue the fight under the guise of self-defense.

One main difference under the laws of the various states is whether the non-aggressor in a fight has a duty to retreat before exercising his or her right to self-defense.

In several cases, the teacher's right of self-defense turned on whether the teacher was much larger in size and weight than the student. The reason for this is, if a teacher is much larger than the student, it might not be reasonable for the teacher to feel threatened by the student's conduct (at least if weapons are not involved).[18]

Many cases also make a distinction between using restraint and "hitting back." It is always best to restrain the student rather than to match blow for blow. The main goal should be to end the disruptive behavior and to protect the teacher and innocent parties, not to harm the student. When a teacher goes beyond restraint and strikes a student, the courts are much more likely to find the teacher went beyond reasonable self-defense measures. This often holds true even when a student is hitting or pushing the teacher. In one case the teacher was pushed twice by a student. The teacher took the student to the principal's office, at which point the student pushed the teacher again. The teacher then hit the student. The court ruled that the teacher could not claim self-defense, noting that the teacher could not reasonably feel threatened by the student's conduct (the teacher was much larger than the student). The court also noted that the teacher could easily have gotten assistance, but did not do so. Finally, there was evidence that, in conversations with other school officials after the incident was over, the teacher never indicated he felt threatened after the student pushed him.[19]

A common denominator in the cases just mentioned is that the student did not use a weapon. When a weapon is involved, the school official has more leeway to use force. In one case, a student swung at a teacher with a 30 inch, 2x4 piece of wood. The teacher fled and returned with a gun. The teacher never pointed the gun but kept it at his side. At the sight of the gun, the student fled. The court held that the teacher was never the aggressor in the affair and defended himself in a reasonable manner when he was physically attacked by a student who was apparently determined to inflict serious injury on the teacher.[20]

State School Violence Statutes

Often in response to the No Child Left Behind Act and other federal legislation, state legislatures have passed laws giving school districts and their employees tools to address the problem of school violence. A common feature of many of these laws is the requirement that the school boards adopt certain policies to deal with violence. Also common to many of these acts is the creation of a centralized information system. Many states have created some type of agency in charge of gathering information on school violence. This agency is often in charge of distributing this information back to the school districts. Some states also require the courts to report students' criminal convictions back to their respective schools so that the administration is aware of who might be a problem.

Most state laws also emphasize the importance of early preventive measures to stop violence. These programs involve a combination of education and counseling. Many programs give teachers the training they need to spot troubled behavior and give students the support they need before problems result in violence. Finally, most of these programs emphasize the importance of getting parents involved.

A final common element of these laws is that the legislature often leaves a large amount of discretion in fashioning rules with the school district at the local level.

Let's look at four sample laws which have been passed in the last ten years or so.

California

The State of California has developed an extensive educational code which fosters safety of schools systems in the state. Several titles of that code are devoted to school violence. The School Safety and Violence Prevention Program is probably the most important measure.[21] California leaves less discretion to local school boards than some other states. Schools must submit their plans to promote safety in order to be eligible for state funding.

Two of the eligibility conditions include the following:

- The school has developed a safety plan.

- The school can demonstrate an ability to carry out a comprehensive school safety and violence prevention strategy.

According to the guidelines published by the California State Board of Education, a disciplinary policy should include a description of specific disruptive behaviors that interfere with the classroom learning environment. Examples given include antisocial behaviors, gang-related attire, excessive absences, and tardiness. The Board has published some "sample" policies that the individual school boards might use when constructing their codes of student conduct.

California also has adopted additional statutes specifically designed to alleviate the problem of gang violence in schools. The legislature enacted this law to inform teachers and school officials what to look for and how to deal with gang activity.[22]

Illinois

Illinois has adopted two approaches to the problem of violence in public schools. The first of these is the establishment of the Illinois Violence Prevention Authority. The Authority is designed to develop a statewide plan to stop school violence in a number of different areas, including public schools. The second approach is violence and anti-bias education. The intent of this program is to educate children at an early age on how to peacefully resolve disputes and thus limit violence.

In 1993 the Illinois legislature enacted a violence and conflict education program.[23] The program requires all school districts to provide instruction in violence prevention and conflict resolution education for grades four through twelve.

Additionally, the Illinois State Board of Education is required to make these violence education materials available to all Illinois public schools. The Illinois State Board of Education website has an extensive manual on school safety that guides school officials in determining the potential areas of concern at their school. The manual was originally published in 1999 and appears to have been periodically updated.[24]

Another related program established to stop school violence is the anti-bias education program. The goal of this program is to "improve inter-group relations on and beyond the school campus".[25]

New York

The state of New York has enacted one of the most extensive school violence laws requiring adherence to a specific code of conduct and providing a uniform violent incident reporting system.

Its state law requires that every school district adopt and maintain a code of conduct for students on school property.[26] The law requires that the code include standards and procedures to ensure security and safety of students and school personnel. It also requires that the code include disciplinary measures to be taken in incidents involving the possession or use of weapons, the use of physical force and threats of violence. Other requirements include provisions for detention, suspension and removal for other acts violating the code, and procedures for reporting and investigating violations. Each code must set forth guidelines on when law enforcement and parents will be notified of certain events. The codes must set forth the circumstances under which a complaint will be filed in criminal court or in juvenile court. The codes must establish minimum suspension periods for repeat offenders who are substantially disruptive of the educational process, or who substantially interfere with the teacher's authority over the classroom. Each district must present their code to the State Board of Education for review. Model codes are available from State authorities. A review of a sampling of local codes reveals they are probably taken from a template.

New York law also requires schools to develop a school safety plan.[27] Such plans must include policies and procedures for responding to implied or direct threats of violence by students, teachers, other school personnel as well as visitors to the school. They also must include policies and procedures for responding to acts of violence, including consideration of zero-tolerance policies for school violence. Such plans must also provide for prevention and intervention strategies such as collaboration with law enforcement, non-violent conflict resolution training, peer mediation programs, and youth courts.

The plans must be reviewed on an annual basis by the school safety team and updated as needed. If a school district fails to adopt a satisfactory code of conduct, the Commissioner may withhold monies from the district.

New York law also requires the Commissioner to establish a statewide uniform violent incident reporting system which all school districts must follow. This law requires the school district to report each violent incident and discuss whether disciplinary action and/or referral to law enforcement occurred.[28] Individual schools can access the database created so they can know any violent history of their students, even if the offense occurred at another school district in the state.

New York law requires courts which have sentenced a student for a crime to report that sentence to the student's school.[29]

Texas

The Texas legislature has adopted a number of bills to curb

the pattern of school violence. One of these legislative initiatives is the establishment of the Texas School Safety Center. The purpose of this Center is to provide school districts and officials with information to stop school violence. Texas also requires that every school board publish an annual report that documents what school violence programs have been implemented. Texas also (like many other states) requires the courts to report convictions of students to the student's school.[30]

The Texas School Safety Center was established in 2001, with the goal of establishing a central research and training center to stop violence in public schools.[31] The law requires the Center to develop and maintain an interactive website with safety information and updates, and upcoming conferences and events. Additionally, the Center publicly recognizes schools which have implemented effective school violence prevention programs.[32]

In an effort to make public schools more accountable for monitoring and preventing violence, the Texas legislature requires each district to publish an annual performance report. One portion of that report gives the state an update on the district's violence prevention policies and programs which implement those policies.[33]

Oklahoma

The Oklahoma Legislature has adopted a number of provisions which give local school boards the authority to both take preventative measures to curb school violence and to respond appropriately to situations involving school violence. Each county school board is given the opportunity to establish its unique set of rules and regulations.

School boards in Oklahoma are authorized to take a number of preventative measures. One provision allows them to contract with licensed professional counselors, social workers and community-based service providers to assist students who might otherwise become violent. [34]

Another provision of Oklahoma law mandates that each school board establish a "Safe School Committee" composed of at least three teachers and three parents. The Committee is to consider problems of violence facing the schools and to work to maintain a safer educational system. The Committee is to compile a list of their findings and submit it to the state.[35]

Another provision of the law requires that each school district develop a disciplinary policy which prohibits bullying, harassment, intimidation and violence, and provides penalties for such behaviors. The law also states that school policies address prevention and education about such matters.[36]

Significantly, the law provides that a teacher shall have the same right as a parent or guardian to control and discipline the student according to district policies while the child is in attendance or in transit to or from the school, or any other school function authorized by the school district or classroom presided over by the teacher.[37]

Students found in possession of a firearm on school property (including school vehicles) must be suspended for a period of not less than one year.[38] Each school district is to publish a policy regarding other offenses, including violent offenses, meriting suspension.

Local School District Codes of Conduct

The No Child Left Behind Act leaves a great amount of discretion in the hands of the individual states to handle problems of school violence. The reaction of the states has been to provide some guidance for the individual school districts in writing a code of student conduct or behavior; to formalize a list of prohibited behaviors; and the punishment for engaging in those behaviors. The guidance ranges from the very specific to the very general. Some states have created model codes. Others have left it up to the individual districts to fashion codes. If your school district has such a code, *it is your best source of information on violence prevention and dealing with violence.* It is also important that you are thoroughly familiar with your local code because, as pointed out elsewhere, if you are acting in conformity with the code, you chances of incurring legal liability are minimized. Conversely, if you are acting outside the code or in a manner prohibited by the code, you increase the chances of being sued individually.

If your school district does not have a code, you should work through your administration or your union to get one published. When the rules are known, well-written, and understandable, everyone benefits.

It might be helpful to look at some selected code provisions to help you get a feel for what they say. For instance, the Longwood Central School District (Suffolk County, New York) Code of Conduct was published in 2003. It contains definitions of various significant terms such as "disruptive student,[39]" "school property,[40]" and "corporal punishment.[41]" The Longwood Code also contains a definition of "violent student." A violent student means a student under the age of 21 who: (1) commits an act of violence upon a school employee, or attempts to do so; (2) commits, while on school property or at a school function or while using school-provided transportation, an act of violence upon another student or any other person on school property or at a school function, or attempts to do so; (3) possesses a weapon while on school property or at a school function; (4) displays, while on school property or at a school function, what appears to be a weapon; (5) threatens, while on school property or at a school function, to use a weapon; (6) knowingly and intentionally damages or destroys the personal property of any school employee or any other person on school property or at a school function; or (7) knowingly and intentionally damages or destroys school district property.

The Longwood code defines responsibilities of students, teachers, administrators and parents and sets forth various rules, the violation of which will result in disciplinary sanctions. Included in the list is injuring another person, threatening injury, destruction of property, arson, bomb threats, bullying, intimidation, extortion, insubordination and inciting discord. The Code makes it clear that behavior on school buses is regulated by the Code just as if the conduct occurred in a classroom.

The Longwood Code states that all students should report violations of the Code. It further states that when staff who are authorized to impose discipline observes an individual engaging in prohibited conduct, and in his or her judgment, it does not pose an immediate threat of injury to persons or property, he/she shall tell the individual that the conduct is prohibited and attempt to persuade the individual to stop the conduct, including a warning of the consequences of failing to stop. If the person refuses to stop, or if the person's conduct poses an immediate threat of injury to person or property, the staff member, shall have the individual immediately removed from school property or the school function. Local law enforcement will be called if necessary.

Staff without disciplinary authority who observe such conduct are to promptly report the conduct to their supervisor.

The Code provides that any weapon, alcohol, or illegal substance should be immediately confiscated so long as the taking of such items does not pose a risk of imminent danger to the person taking the item.

The Code requires that law enforcement must be notified of any Code violation which constitutes a crime and substantially affects the order or security of the school. The notification should occur as soon as practical but in no event later that the close of the business day on which the official learns of the violation.

The Code encourages teachers to first use "time-honored classroom management techniques" in an attempt to control most situations. These include sending the student to a "timeout," sending him/her to the principal, or sending him/her to a counselor. The Code authorizes a classroom teacher to remove a disruptive student for up to two days. This may take place only after an informal discussion between student and teacher where the student is allowed to explain his or her version of relevant events. If the student poses a danger or ongoing threat of disruption, the teacher may order the student to be removed immediately. In this case, the teacher must explain to the student why he/she is being removed and give the student a chance to present his/her version of events within 24 hours.

Students who bring a weapon to school shall be suspended for a year. Students who commit other violent acts will be suspended for a minimum of five days. There are special rules for dealing with students with disabilities who commit violent acts.

Riverside Public School District 96 (Cook County, Illinois) also has published an extensive code entitled Philosophy of Student Behavior. This code defines bullying as *any act, speech, or expression intended to injure or intimidate another.* Bullying is strictly prohibited by the code. The display of gang dress or symbols also is banned.

The code also sets forth teacher rights and responsibilities. The teacher has the right and the responsibility to maintain order. The code goes on to state that in all disciplinary incidents, due process will be observed. This basically includes (1) advising the student of the reason for suspension; (2) allowing the student to respond to the suspension by presenting evidence; (3) written notice to the parents; (4) the right to appeal.

Texas has published a Model Student Code of Conduct for use by school districts in that state. Although the preface to the Code recites that it is intended only to assist the district in developing and maintaining a local code, there is not much left for the local district to do.

It is noteworthy that the Model Code asserts that the school district has jurisdiction over any act occurring at a school function, regardless of location. Undoubtedly, most districts in the country would agree. The Code goes on to state that any time a threat is made against a school or school employee, the district will have jurisdiction to impose discipline regardless of where the threat was made. The code provides that the district has the right to search any vehicle on school premises whenever there is reasonable cause to believe it contains articles or materials prohibited by the district. The district reserves similar rights when it comes to inspecting student lockers.

General conduct violations include insubordination, fighting, bullying, harassment, sexual harassment, hazing, possessing weapons (including "look-alike" weapons), verbal exchanges that threaten the safety of another student, and disruptive activities. Bullying is defined as a written or oral expression or physical conduct that a school district's board of trustees or the board's designee determines (1) to have the effect of physically harming a student, damaging a student's property, or placing a student in reasonable fear of harm, or (2) to be sufficiently severe, persistent, or pervasive to create an intimidating, threatening, or abusive educational environment for a student.

Hazing is defined as an intentional or reckless act, on or off campus, by one person alone or acting with others, that endangers the mental or physical health or safety of a student for the purpose of pledging, initiation into, affiliation with, holding office in, or maintaining membership in an organization.

The Ability to Search

Statutes (both state and federal), the common law, and local school codes give us many useful tools for dealing with violence and potentially violent situations. An additional tool, and one which is regulated by all of the previously-mentioned sources of rules, is the ability to search.

If you think a student has a gun, bomb, or other weapon in a purse, locker, or backpack, what is the school's right to search?

You should be very familiar with your school's policy in this area, because not all school employees have the right to conduct the search themselves. Still, it will help you to know what can and cannot be done in this area because, even though you may not be able to do it yourself, you can always bring the matter to the attention of someone who does have the authority to conduct a search. Many states have laws which govern this area as well. Most of these laws are just common sense, but you need to check to see if your state has such a law.

The main rule pertaining to school searches, no matter where you are, is that the search must be reasonable. What does this mean?

In 1985, the United States Supreme Court decided the case of *New Jersey v. T.L.O.*[42] In this case the high Court gave school officials more latitude to search than other governmental officials, such as the police, for example. In all events the school official must have a *reasonable suspicion* that the student has violated a school rule *and that the evidence of such violation is in the place to be searched.* When the school official is acting to uphold school discipline in order to insure an effective learning environment (as opposed to enforcing the criminal law), more leeway is given to the amount of intrusion in a search.

Another aspect of the reasonableness inquiry is that the search must be reasonably related to its purpose. For instance, if you are looking for a rifle, you would not be permitted to search a purse. On the other hand, if you were looking for a pistol, you may well be able to search a purse. In all events, you must be looking for something that it is illegal for the student to have, or the possession of which violates school rules or constitutes a danger or is stolen property.

A third aspect to the reasonableness requirement is that the information which gives you reasonable suspicion must be recent. If a student tells you they saw a knife in a student's locker a year ago, this may not give you reasonable suspicion that the knife is still there.

Usually, local laws and rules will allow searches to be conducted not only on school premises, but on buses and at school functions. Some laws require the search to be conducted by a person of the same sex as the person being searched and witnessed. Other laws say that this must be done only "if practicable." According to the *T.L.O.* case, school officials must take into consideration the age and sex of the student as well as the nature of the suspected infraction.

Most laws prohibit strip searches of a student and prohibit the removal of any clothing except cold weather outerwear. Other states permit the search of pockets and to require the student to remove his/her shoes.

You should determine if your district has policies specifically informing students that they have no expectation of privacy in lockers, desks, or other school property. In many states, districts which have such policies are not even required to have reasonable suspicion in order to search lockers, desks and other school property. A search of a locker, therefore, could occur at any time and for no reason at all.[43] Many districts conduct random searches of lockers and desks. Some rules state that the examination must occur in the presence of a witness.

Many search policies and statutes allow student vehicles to be searched based on reasonable suspicion while parked on school property. In other words, there must be reasonable cause to believe that the vehicle contains contraband or weapons. Usually, a reasonable effort to locate the student must be made prior to the search.

One useful pointer is to consider requesting the student's permission to search, if the article is a backpack, vehicle, or some other item of non-school property. If the student consents to the search, then it does not matter if you are able to meet the reasonable suspicion standard. If a person freely consents to a search, they have no standing to later challenge it. If the student refuses, you may proceed with the search as long as you have met the reasonable suspicion requirements.

Corporal Punishment

Some state statutes allow for the use of moderate corporal punishment in schools. Of course, the provisions of the various statutes will control your actions in your particular state. In some states, parental consent is required, although it has been held that such consent is not constitutionally mandated. Most states ban corporal punishment, although a few of these states allow exceptions for quelling a disturbance, self-defense, defense of others, to obtain possession of a weapon or other dangerous device. The first state to ban corporal punishment was New Jersey, in 1867. The most recent statute banning corporal punishment was Delaware in 2003. In several states where corporal punishment is not banned by the state, local school districts have rules banning or regulating corporal punishment. Please refer to the chart at the end of this chapter for a state-by-state summary of corporal punishment laws. Remember, this chart was accurate as of the time of publication, but the information could be outdated if a state has modified its law in the interim.

Usually, there is not requirement to give the student any kind of hearing or due process right before administering corporal punishment, but a hearing may be held afterwards on whether the punishment was proper under all of the circumstances of the case. Remember, when you act to physically discipline a student, you are acting as an agent of the school district and not just as a substitute for the parent.

In those states where corporal punishment is allowed, there are several factors which determine whether it should be used:

- The force is used as a means of discipline.

- The force is not excessive.

- It was administered in good faith and not out of anger or malice.

- It is consistent with the local school board's disciplinary policy.

- The official is not acting for personal motives.

Once again, it seems that the rule of common sense is at the bottom of most decisions on the use of corporal punishment. It is also true that you will not be judged as harshly if you make a mistake in making a spur-of-the-moment decision. You must act in furtherance of discipline, not because you are angry. Corporal punishment should always be used as a last resort, when lesser forms of punishment are not likely to remedy the situation, or where such other forms of punishment have been tried and failed to correct the problem.

Remember, some studies show that physical violence against children encourages them to be violent in return. Such children may grow to be adults who are less likely to be able to solve problems without resorting to violence. Other writers note that the existence of corporal punishment in the classroom leads to absenteeism and dropouts. Thus, in addition to the legal reasons for avoiding corporal punishment except as a last resort (where legally permitted), there are non-legal reasons pointing to its lack of effectiveness.

A key factor in whether corporal punishment is deemed reasonable is whether it is administered to restore control and order or is it administered merely to punish. If it is the latter, then the school district (and the teacher) may be in trouble. *Corporal punishment should be meted out only when necessary to keep order, and lesser forms of punishment are inadequate.*

Indeed, experience teaches us that verbal reprimands and warnings should resolve most situations (although — admittedly — not all of them). For those situations in the minority, only the minimal amount of force should be used to restore order. For instance, grabbing a student who is about to damage property may be reasonable, but hitting that student would not be. Subduing a student who is using force or about to use force on a fellow student or teacher would be another example of where force is reasonable under the circumstances.

Remember, corporal punishment and other use of force should be used only to regain control of the classroom or the school environment. If you do not need to engage in corporal punishment or use force – refrain. Never let your anger get the better of you.

Finally, teachers who "go ballistic" on a student may lose their immunity from being sued individually. Most states do not provide immunity for "willful and wanton" conduct.

Remedies of the Injured School Employee against the School District

What remedy does a school employee who is injured by a student have against the school district? In most states, the exclusive remedy for the school employee is to file a claim under the state's workers compensation statute. This is the same law a worker hurt in a factory by a piece of falling pipe would use, for instance. It does not matter if the worker himself or herself was at fault in the accident, they will receive compensation. It also does not matter if the employer was somehow at fault (or not at fault), the worker's recovery will still be limited to workers compensation.

Workers Compensation benefits usually entail payment of all medical expenses, payments while a worker is temporarily disabled from work and, in some cases, payment for permanent disability or death. There are no punitive damages, damages for pain and suffering or mental anguish.

Thus, if a student hits a teacher and injures him or her, the teacher will of course have a remedy at law against the student in the way of a civil lawsuit. Naturally, criminal charges can be filed subject to the state's laws on crimes committed by juveniles.

The main exception to the above rule comes into play when it is alleged that the employer intentionally injured the worker. In such cases, the employee may sue the employer for a tort, such as assault and battery. Negligence on the part of the employer, however, is not enough in most states in order for the employee to be able to sue.

For instance, in one case a student intentionally threw a rock and hit the teacher in the head causing injuries. The teacher sued the child, his parents, and the school district. The school district defended stating that workers compensation was the teacher's exclusive remedy. The teacher countered by asserting that the school district knew of the student's propensity to commit assaults and failed to take any steps to prevent the student from committing assaults. The court sided with the school district, stating that where the failings of the school district were merely negligent (as opposed to intent to harm the teacher), the teacher's exclusive remedy is worker compensation.[44]

In another case, a teacher was sexually assaulted by one of the students. The student had actually told the school district (before the assault) that he could not control his impulses. The school failed to warn the teacher. The teacher sued the school district, claiming that it intentionally failed to maintain a safe workplace, and its actions created a situation where injury was substantially certain to occur. The court disagreed, stating that the school district's failure to warn or take any other measures, while negligent, did not amount to an intent to injury the teacher.[45]

Certainly, where there is no allegation of negligence on the part of the school district, there can be no argument that there is a remedy other than that of worker's compensation. For instance, in a case where a teacher was injured breaking up a fight, workers compensation was ruled to be the teacher's exclusive remedy.[46]

In order for the harm to be intentionally caused by the school district, most states require there be a showing that some official of the district had a subjective intent to harm the teacher or other school employee. Other states, in addition to making an exception for subjective intent to harm, also will deem the employer intended to harm the employee when (1) the employer had actual knowledge that an injury was **certain** to occur and (2) the employer *willfully* disregarded that knowledge.[47] This also is a very difficult standard to meet. Note that the school district must be proved to have had actual knowledge that an injury was going to happen. Further, you must show more than the school district was negligent in what it did with that knowledge, but also must show it willfully ignored the situation. An example might be if the assistant principal saw a student with a gun headed to class who said he was going to kill his teacher and the official did nothing even though he had it in his power to call for assistance.

In most situations, the teacher is free to sue the student causing the injury and also can file a worker's compensation claim against the school district. Suit typically is not available in most states, if the person causing the injury is a co-worker. There are a few close cases where it is alleged that the student also was working as an employee of the school.[48] In most situations, however, the teacher is free to bring a civil action against the student.

Status of Corporal Punishment in the Fifty States
(Current as of July 13, 2006)

STATE	STATUS	STATE	STATUS
Alabama	allowed	Montana	banned
Alaska	banned	Nebraska	banned
Arizona	allowed	Nevada	banned
Arkansas	allowed	New Hampshire	banned
California	banned	New Jersey	banned
Colorado	allowed	New Mexico	allowed
Connecticut	banned	New York	banned
Delaware	banned	North Carolina	allowed
District of Columbia	banned	North Dakota	banned
Florida	allowed	Ohio	allowed
Georgia	allowed	Oklahoma	allowed
Hawaii	banned	Oregon	banned
Idaho	allowed	Pennsylvania	allowed
Illinois	banned	Rhode Island*	banned
Indiana	allowed	South Carolina	allowed
Iowa	banned	South Dakota	banned
Kansas	allowed	Tennessee	allowed
Kentucky	allowed	Texas	allowed
Louisiana	allowed	Utah	banned
Maine	banned	Vermont	banned
Maryland	banned	Virginia	banned
Massachusetts	banned	Washington	banned
Michigan	banned	West Virginia	banned
Minnesota	banned	Wisconsin	banned
Missouri	banned	Wyoming	allowed
Mississippi	allowed		

* Rhode Island does not have a state statute that bans corporal punishment at schools, but all of the school districts in Rhode Island ban corporal punishment.

ENDNOTES

1 *Davis v. Monroe County School Board*, 526 U.S. 629(1999)
2 *Collins v. City of Harker Heights*, 503 U.S. 115 (1992)
3 *Mirand v. City of New York*, 637 N.E.2d 263 (N.Y. 1994)
4 *Ohman v. Board of Education of City of New York*, 90 N.E.2d 474 (N.Y. 1949)
5 *Randell v. Tulsa Independent School Dist. No.1*, 889 P.2d 1266 (Okla. App. 1994)
6 *Truitt v. Diggs*, 611 P.2d 633 (Okla. 1980)
7 *Castaldo v. Jefferson County Sheriff et al.*, 192 F.Supp. 2d 1124 (D. Colo. 2001)a
8 489 U.S. 189
9 *Doe v. Hillsboro Indep. Sch. Dist.*, 113 F.3d 1412 (5th Cir. 1997); *Dorothy J. v. Little Rock Sch. Distr.*, 7 F.3d 729(double check this cite)(8th Cir. 1993); *Maldonado v. Josey*, 975 F.2d 727 (10th Cir. 1992).
10 *Kneipp v. Tedder*, 95 F.3d 1199 (3rd Cir. 1996)
11 *Sutton v. Utah State School for the Deaf & Blind*, 173 F.3d 1226 (10th Cir. 1999)
12 *Ireland v. Jefferson County Sheriff's Department et al.*, 193 F.Supp. 2d 1201 (D. Colo. 2002)
13 20 U.S.C. Section 8921
14 20 U.S.C. Section 6311 et seq.
15 20 U.S.C. Section 7151
16 20 U.S.C. Section 6314
17 20 U.S.C. Section 7115
18 *Bivins v. Unemployment Compensation Board of Review*, 470 A.2d 662 (pa. Cmw1th. 1984).
19 *Parham v. Raleigh County Bd. Of Education*, 192 W.Va. 540(W.Va. 1994).
20 *Landry v. Ascension Parish School Board*, 415 So.2d 473 (La. App. 1982).
21 Cal. Educ. Code, Section 35924.11
22 Cal. Educ. Code, Section 51264
23 105 Ill. Compo Stat. Ann. 5/27-23.4
24 http://ceep.crc. uiuc.edu/ eecearchive/ digests/ 1992/hohens92.html
25 105 Ill. Compo Stat. Ann. 5/27-23.6
26 N.Y. Educ. Law, Section 2801
27 N.Y. Educ. Law, Section 2801-a
28 N.Y. Educ. Law, Section 2802
29 N.Y. Crim. Proced., Section 380.90
30 Tex. Criminal Code, Section 15.27
31 Tex. Educ. Code, Section 37.202
32 *Id.*

[33] Tex. Educ. Code, Section 39.053
[34] 70 Oklahoma Statutes, Section 24-100.1
[35] 70 Oklahoma Statutes, Section 24-100.5
[36] 70 Oklahoma Statutes, Section 24-100.4
[37] *Id.*
[38] 70 Oklahoma Statutes, Section 24-101.3
[39] Disruptive Student means an elementary or secondary student under the age of 21 who, while on school property or attending a school function, demonstrates a persistent unwillingness to comply with the teacher's instructions or repeatedly violates the teacher's classroom behavior rules or this Code, is substantially disruptive of the educational process, substantially interferes with the teacher's authority over the class, or conducts himself/herself in a manner that intrudes upon or endangers the freedom, health or safety of self or others.
[40] School property means any building, structure, athletic playing field, playground, parking lot or land contained within the real property boundary line of a public elementary or secondary school, or on any other property owned by the school district, or in or on a school bus or other school provided transportation.
[41] Corporal punishment is any act of physical force upon a student for the purpose of punishing that student.
[42] 469 U.S. 325
[43] See, for example, "Student Responsibilities and Rights," published by Fairfax County (Virginia) Public Schools, August 2004.
[44] *Hal/iman v. Los Angeles Unified School Dist.,* 163 Cal. App.3d 46 (Cal. App. 1984).
[45] *Simpson v. State,* 998 S.W.2d 304 (Tex. App. 1999).
[46] *Scionti v. Board of Education,* 225 A.D.2d 537 (N.Y. App. Div. 1996).
[47] *Vallandingham v. Clover Park School District No. 400,* 109 P.3d 805 (Wash. 2005).
[48] *Mitchell v. Gamble,* 86 P.3d 944 (Az. App. 2004).

PART II

The Role of Child Development, Behavior and Learning in the Prevention of School Violence

There is a consensus within the United States that we are a very violent people. International statistics indicate that this country is the most murderous of any developed nation on earth. The estimated homicide rate in this country is one for each 100,000 persons. The yearly total is approximately 20 to 25,000 murders. Rates for other aggressive crimes, including armed robbery, non-lethal assault and rape, also are significantly greater than are those for comparable Western European societies.

In spite of statistics that indicate the total crime rate in the United States has declined in recent years, there is a widely held belief within this country that violence in schools has increased dramatically. This concern focuses not only on physical assaults and homicides that have garnered national attention, but also on lesser forms of violence of increasing concern to parents, teachers, law enforcement, school administrators, legislators and citizens. These include acts of verbal harassment, theft and vandalism.

Concern on the part of parents and school employees has precipitated a *"No Tolerance"* policy for violent and abusive behaviors, together with an increased vigilance on the part of parents, teachers, day care workers, coaches and other adults who work in a surrogate or supervisory capacity with children and youth. Physical, verbal, sexual, and emotional abuse are no longer considered to be "just a part of growing up." This lower tolerance for violence reflects a greater awareness of its presence. This, along with an increasing concern for both the immediate and long-range physical, emotional, and psychological harm that is the consequence of violence.

There also is a belief that children are exhibiting aggressive behaviors at earlier ages. Factors cited as contributors (if not causes) for this phenomenon include:

- Themes of physical violence and sexual exploitation on TV, movies, cartoons, video tapes, computer games, and print media.

- Glorification of violence as an indication of strength and courage in the legitimate defense of self or others.

- Widely held acceptance of sports-related aggression as acceptable; even heroic.

- Deterioration in the quality of family life, with less time spent in shared activities.

To date, most public efforts to address violence by children have been ineffective. Exceptions are programs that coordinate the efforts of schools, churches, and other community service agencies at the neighborhood level. These integrated programs engender greater vigilance by parents, teachers, and others who supervise children.

They include extensive training in violence prevention and conflict resolution training. They also have addressed needs for environmental modifications. They define effective emergency interventions. Few have examined the effects of normal development on the thinking, behaviors, and social interactions of school-age children.

At an individual level, most parents accept their responsibilities to foster social development in their children. They understand that the role of parenting typically spans several life stages. They realize that exceptions vary according to the child's physical, cognitive, social, ethical and emotional development.

Thus, the specific demands are different for pre-school children as compared to those in high school. Basic research in child development indicates the following:

- Wholesome, age-appropriate activities, experiences and limitations are essential to the "internalization of boundaries" and the acquisition of those self-management skills so essential to adaptation and problem-solving at each stage of life.

  The basis for this sense of competence lies in the belief that she/he can learn and effectively use these basic skills. Because these skills are hierarchical, mastery of one set of developmental tasks is essential to success at the next "task level."

- Language is the primary system for both thought and its communication. Without language, thinking and behaviors are chaotic and fragmented. Observations and analysis of children's behaviors have identified distinct changes in their thinking and problem-solving as they mature. In normal children, there is a transition from literal, concrete and simplistic views of personal and social events to sophisticated reasoning analysis.

  This sophisticated reasoning analysis permits increasingly astute examination of experiences as well as the ability to generate effective responses. The understanding and application of these theories permits effective communication, because it allows us to talk with children in a format that is readily useable to them.

Chapter Four

Development Principles: Infancy, Early Childhood and Adolescence

---

Within each developmental stage, there are identifiable physical, cognitive, behavioral, social, emotional and cultural skills a child must acquire to be competent and to advance to the next, more complex level. These skills form the basis for a positive self-concept and a sense of competence. Each stage of development requires mastery of a number of essential tasks.

Mastery at one level is essential to success at the next. Failure to master early developmental skills in ways that permit healthy social, emotional and cognitive growth leads to maladaptive behaviors. These become increasingly ingrained and debilitating over time. If allowed to persist, they precipitate and support asocial or anti-social behaviors.

Research data support the premise that traumatic experiences in pre-verbal children cause disruptions in normal developmental processes. These studies cast doubt on the commonly held notion that children are immune to emotional trauma they observe or experience prior to verbal language acquisition. Rather, this research strongly suggests that traumatic, preverbal experiences taint a child's perception of, and reactions to his/her environment and those within it. In this way, pre-verbal experiences cause a child to be less trusting, as well as more wary and anxious.

Ineffective parenting also contributes to emotional and behavior disorders in children. Many parents of these children do not discriminate among age-appropriate, abnormal and socially unacceptable actions. These parents tend to be inconsistent in their expectations as well as in the care of their offspring. Thus, they do not provide appropriate guidance and supervision. Often, they expect adult levels of performance and self-management without the benefit of maturity, modeling and guidance. These parents also tend to be overly punitive when a child fails to meet unrealistic expectations.

One key developmental task is learning to control socially inappropriate impulses and behavior. When significant adults (parents, teachers and extended family members) do not consistently teach and reward developmentally appropriate skills, they create confusion and facilitate behaviors that impede (rather than support) continued social, emotional and behavioral development.

Thus, children living in chaotic, inconsistent environments often exhibit difficulty attaining age-appropriate, normative behavior patterns and skills. Many adapt poorly to structural routines and resent limits. They challenge rules and are slow to internalize effective self-management controls. They are strident in demanding respect for their own rights, but have little respect for the rights of others. They resent accountability, limits and other forms of external control. They perceive minimal demands as infringements on their autonomy. These children are more likely than others to use aggression, tantrums, threats and other similarly maladaptive behaviors that do not support social, emotional and behavioral development. Often, they form peer groups that harass and intimidate others. They avoid tasks that are physically and/or cognitively demanding.

Frequently, these children also exhibit a limited capacity to sustain attention, concentration and effort. They are disruptive in school. They adapt poorly to school routines and have difficulty making friends. They challenge rules and are slow to internalize controls. They fight rather than negotiate. They do not profit from developmentally appropriate learning activities. They do not invest in learning. They do not persist, even in activities they profess to enjoy. They do not respond well to praise with enhanced self-esteem, but may modify their behaviors to earn tangible rewards. By adolescence, a high number of these aggressive, disruptive children engage in delinquent, anti-social, sometimes criminal behaviors. Most common are truancy, theft, vandalism and assault.

Teachers and therapists who serve as surrogate parents to children who exhibit severe learning and behavior problems note a higher than average incidence of violence, sexual abuse, illicit drug use and lawlessness among their parents and extended families. Those who attempt to teach and guide children who experience this type of dysfunctional environment note ineffective learning strategies, expectations of success with minimal success, and a very limited capacity to sustain effort in the face of difficulty. Just like their children, these parents and other family members frequently lack the basic social and interpersonal skills needed to be effective parents. These parents tend to be inconsistent, and sometimes self-serving in their expectations, but in turn neglectful of their own responsibilities to nurture and mold their children's behaviors.

Inadequate parents are the exception, not the norm. Most adults accept their responsibilities to foster normative social development in their children. They understand these commitments span several stages in the child's life. Most adults also recognize that expectations within each of these stages vary accordingly to the child's physical, cognitive-intellectual, social, spiritual and emotional development.

Thus, while there are expectations that all parents will foster social adaptation in their child or children, the specific demands of that task are quite different for parents of a pre-school child as compared to one in high school. When parents do not model, teach and reward age-appropriate effective, social and self-management skills, they may unknowingly encourage behaviors that are maladaptive. As a consequence, their children exhibit difficulty acquiring age-appropriate behavior patterns and social skills.

Child development specialists note that even *young* children who live in chaotic, inconsistent environments exhibit difficulty attaining age-appropriate, normative behavior patterns and social skills. They adapt poorly to home and school routines, have difficulty making friends; challenge rules, and are slow to internalize controls. Research that attempts to identify family and community dynamics that contribute to atypical and anti-social behaviors in children has identified needs to be strong, self-reliant and brave.

Easy access to weapons and the powerful image they hold is a second disruptive factor. The combination of the availability of weapons, vicarious violent experiences, and the glamorization of aggression as a means of solving problems and reconcile differences is a particularly potent source of violent behaviors in school-age children.

A Summary of Developmental Principles

1. Normal development from birth to adulthood requires mastery of well-defined physical, cognitive and social-emotional skills. Each stage of development includes specific, essential developmental tasks.

2. Development occurs in identifiable stages. In each, there are physical, personal, behavioral, social and cultural skills that every child must master to be competent and advance to the next, more complex level.

3. The basis for a positive self-concept is supportive feedback from parents and other significant individuals in the child's life.

4. Physical development requires adequate nutrition, exercise, sleep, stimulation, medical treatment and a healthy life style.

5. Healthy social-emotional development requires meaningful human interactions.

6. The basis for a positive self-concept is the belief that one can acquire and use the skills needed for success in life.

7. Failure to master early developmental skills in a way that permits growth causes maladaptive feelings, attitudes, beliefs and behaviors that become increasingly obvious and ingrained over time.

8. Effective interpersonal skills and behaviors are essential for success in life. If not addressed in positive and constructive ways, maladaptive feelings, attitudes, beliefs and behaviors precipitate and support psychiatric conditions that preclude normal social-emotional functioning as an adult.

Chapter Five

The Developmental Stages

Jean Piaget defines stages of development that range from birth to adulthood. Each stage is characterized by its own specific physical, sensory motor and cognitive skills and behaviors. Let's review them for a better understanding of the students discussed in this book.

Sensorimotor Period

Infancy spans the period from birth to about two years of age. This developmental period is characterized by rapid physical maturation. During this time, children experience physical and cognitive changes that are necessary for survival and that permit increasing autonomy and mobility. These include the abilities to suck, grasp, focus, gaze and track within a limited visual field. Initially, an infant responds only to its internal states and objects within its immediate sensorimotor experiences.

Infants lack a sense of object constancy. The child has no sense that an object or person continues to exist outside his/her immediate environment. Thus, if the child's mother leaves his/her immediate sensory boundaries, the child does not realize that the mother continues to exist. If the infant drops an object, he/she does not search for it.

As children continue to develop, they refine these basic sensorimotor skills. They also acquire and refine more complex cognitive abilities. They coo, then babble, then talk. They roll, then crawl, then walk. Physical development in fine motor coordination permits both grasp and release. Refinements in vision and memory allow them to discriminate familiar from unfamiliar people.

At about seven months, a child begins to seek contact with objects of attachment. She/he scoots, rolls and crawls so they are more mobile within their immediate environment. The child actively explores their surroundings and seeks physical contact. These activities reflect cognitive maturation in that they reflect a rudimentary awareness of object constancy.

By the time a child begins walking, he/she uses a number of different behaviors to influence caretakers, control the environment, and satisfy their needs. Critical developmental tasks within this first two years of life include:

- Formation of bonds with caregivers that support a sense of trust and feelings of emotional security.

- Refinement of basic sensory and motor skills that encourage and permit exploration of the child's immediate environment.

- Acquisition of object constancy. That is, the knowledge that an object may exist outside the child's immediate visual field. Effective parenting demands:

    - Structuring a safe, stimulating environment.
    - Redirection to prevent physical harm.
    - Emotional support in times of distress.

Verbal abuse is emotionally harmful. Physical punishment is *never* appropriate.

Pre-operational Period (Toddler-Preschool)

Children in the age range of two to six or seven years typically are impulsive and self-centered. Two-year-olds need a rich variety of social and play activities because they are concrete in their thinking. They communicate their feelings and desires through actions, vocalizations and physical gestures. These children are not capable of rational thought or abstract reasoning. Therefore, they do not anticipate consequences in the absence of actual experiences. Their thoughts and ideas are based upon these sensory and motor experiences.

With physical maturity and experience, children begin to associate objects with words, persons, other objects and events. This acquisition of "practical intelligence" is reflected in symbolic and imaginary play. Children remain self-centered in their world view because they cannot engage in abstract problem-solving.

Children in this stage of cognitive development achieve a sense of autonomy and control through fantasy that often includes imaginary friends. They are creative in both play and spoken language. However, often they do not distinguish reality from fantasy. Many have imaginary pets or playmates.

During their third year of life, most of these children begin to use symbolization in both verbal language and in play. They may construct unique words, use common words in unusual ways, or attach uncommon meanings to ordinary language. Conflicts with parents are common. Developmental tasks during this developmental period include the following:

- Acquisition of verbal language to communicate their needs and preferences.

- Problem-solving that is guided by sensory perceptions.

- Imagination that blurs the boundaries between reality and fantasy.

- Symbolization in both play and verbal language.

- Acquisition of rudimentary social skills.

Effective parenting both sets limits and supports the child's need for autonomy. Behavior management strategies must include clear definitions of problem behaviors and consequences. By using these principles, parents teach children to make choices and experience the consequences of their own decisions. As children experience consistency in expectations and outcomes, they acquire an increased sense of security, autonomy and self-reliance. In contrast, punishment based upon threats to withdraw love produces guilt and feelings of anxiety and shame. These disciplinary methods feed anger and rebellion. They undermine autonomy and create dependency.

Pre-Operational (Concrete Operations)

This stage spans the elementary school years (i.e. approximately ages seven to about the twelfth year). Primary school-age children (ages six through eight) typically engage in group activities that include vivid imagination and fantasies. These are an essential tool for learning and socialization. These behaviors and play activities also reflect problem-solving based upon their own experiences.

Primary school-aged children feel empathy for others who have had experiences similar to their own. They do not reason abstractly. They understand being responsible for their own behaviors, but have difficulty conceptualizing outside their own limited range of experiences. Their ideas of social norms are based upon imposed rules rather than internalized values.

Initially both boys and girls in this stage of development are bisexual, in that they can express strong emotional feelings such as admiration, empathy and disdain toward peers of both sexes. During this period, children begin to identify themselves in terms of their sex. They establish same-sex peer relationships, they begin to exhibit a preference for their same-sex parent, siblings, friends and teachers. They also search for clues such as playmates, clothing, preferred activities and interests that are typical of their own sex.

With maturation and experience, primary school age children are increasingly capable of understanding simple, concrete ideas of good and bad. By the time they enter middle school, most understand cause and effect. These children do not always anticipate the consequences of their actions. Cognitive growth is enhanced by parent modeling, discussion and experiences. Therefore, it is essential that parents model the behaviors they wish to teach their children. This can be done by engaging them in discussions about the ethical and moral implications of specific behaviors, and creating environments that reinforce appropriate decisions and actions.

Boys usually have more narrow views of appropriate sex-role behaviors and interests than is typical for girls. Some of these gender differences are rooted in genetic make-up. Others are arbitrary: they reflect social expectations in the absence of an underlying physiological basis. Society typically rewards self-assertiveness, independence, achievement, dominance and experimental learning in boys. It reinforces interpersonal sensitivity, submissiveness and nurturance in girls. Significant deviations from these arbitrary norms often trigger negative reactions from parents, teachers, coaches, and other significant adults.

Social development in middle school children is reflected in cooperation, team play, skill learning, and self-reflection within same sex peer groups. Children learn to contribute to group and team goals. These are critical developmental tasks because they both reflect and demand an increased awareness of social norms.

A child who does not experience recognition, success and failure through such group experiences is at risk for feelings of inferiority, anger and frustration that are often displaced onto the larger community through anti-social attitudes and behaviors.

Failure to master these essential developmental tasks also leads to rejection by peers at a time when children are attempting to learn fundamental social skills needed from this point into adult life. External approval is essential to a positive self-assessment. Within this process of skill acquisition, middle school children often become overly self-critical. It is important that mistakes be used as opportunities to foster learning and provide guidance, rather than condemnation. The wise use of teaching and discipline allows children to maintain a sense of competence when learning from their mistakes.

Middle school children also need adult supervision, encouragement, and approval to invest in activities that are personally and socially worthwhile. Team sports, scouting, and other adult-supervised, community-based, peer group activities provide opportunities to learn and refine these skills. Parent involvement and supervision are critical, not only to ensure good decision-making, but to also mitigate those peer pressures that lead to socially inappropriate activities. Children who do not receive this needed guidance and support often form peer group gangs that reinforce feelings of failure and alienation. These children commit to peer group norms at the expense of autonomy. When such groups lack adult supervision, they often result in anti-social behaviors that cause children to be targets for legal interventions.

Adolescence

Early adolescence brings rapid physical and cognitive changes. With the onset of puberty, both boys and girls must adjust to very significant physical and emotional changes. Disparities amongst peers can cause anxiety in both girls and boys who develop more slowly than is typical of their peers.

These physical changes can include brain maturation that facilitates a greater capacity for logical thinking and analytical problem-solving. However, this increased ability to reason like an adult is limited by a lack of experiences in addressing more complex issues. Because of their relative inexperience, adolescents often resent adult-imposed limitations. Without adequate guidance and boundaries, many adolescents make unwise decisions that have long-term consequences. These include:

- Termination of education without acquiring adequate job skills.

- Choosing friends on the basis of conformity rather then compatibility.

- Engaging in reckless, potentially destructive behaviors.

Significant developmental tasks during this stage of development include:

- Learning to make good choices about critical life issues.

- Resisting impulses and pressures to engage in potentially dangerous or self-destructive behaviors.

- Identifying the limits of one's own abilities.

- Setting and striving for long-term goals.

- Maintaining self-esteem in the face of conflict or controversy with family and friends.

Effective parenting demands the identification of clearly defined consequences of behaviors, while also maintaining a supportive relationship, insisting that the adolescent becomes increasingly responsible for his/her own behaviors. Ineffective parenting can support the adolescent's need for greater autonomy in ways that cause them to experience adult responsibilities as well as physical and/or emotional harm.

Late Adolescence / Early Adulthood

Critical developmental skills during this stage reflect a transition from parental control to autonomy. Critical tasks at this stage include:

- Refinement of sex role identity.

- Internalization of moral principles.

- Wise career choices.

Many young adults continue to be dependent upon their parents until they complete their education, find appropriate work, and establish a home. These developmental tasks often involve education, guidance and experimentation. During this phase, young adults re-examine the social rules and values they learned at home. When parents and other significant adults are understanding, supportive and wise in their guidance, they foster emotional maturity and a sense of responsibility. The absence of mature, adult guidance leads to confusion, and fosters a sense of rebellion that may bear life-long consequences.

Learning Differences Amongst Children

Most children are within normal limits in their physical, cognitive and social development. These children learn and achieve well in typical classrooms. They have friends. They enjoy a wide range of social activities. Other children vary from the normal range so that they have atypical needs and interests.

Gifted Children

These children both learn at accelerated rates and have unique learning styles. If challenged in productive and supportive ways, they excel. If their unique learning needs are not acknowledged and accommodated, they often feel ignored. These children then acquire negative attitudes toward parents, school, teachers, coaches, supervisors and peers. The result can be anger and resentment that is paired with the intelligence needed to plan and carry out harmful actions.

Specific Learning Disabilities

This group of children is essentially normal in physical, cognitive and social development. But, they have specific cognitive difficulties that cause them to learn in unique, unconventional ways. Many of these children are both bright and creative if given opportunities to learn in ways that match their cognitive skills. Most require accommodations to maximize academic learning and performance. These adjustments to classroom routines may include specially trained teachers, extra time to complete assignments and tests, and the use of a calculator and/or audiotape recorder. Factors that exacerbate these learning problems include poorly structured instruction and being socially ostracized.

Attention Deficit Disorder (ADD)

This group of students includes many who are restless, impulsive and/or inattentive. Appropriate medications help most by increasing their capacity to focus and pay attention. Effective interventions both at home and in school include:

- Consistent enforcement of rules.

- Behavior Management to both reward desired behaviors and penalize inappropriate behaviors.

- The wise use of medications.

- Most ADD students require accommodations to maximize their achievements.

Emotional and Behavioral Problems

This group of children typically exhibits significant emotional and behavioral problems. These difficulties often reflect a complex mix of genetic, environmental and learning factors. Many of these children are belligerent, irritable, hostile, argumentative and aggressive. Others are emotionally withdrawn, anxious, passive and non-communicative. Still others are self-centered, manipulative and emotionally distant. Some exhibit clearly abnormal ideas, beliefs and behaviors. They all tend to interact in ways not appropriate to given situations. Many vacillate with respect to their moods and willingness to interact with others. Most become irritable and resistant when demands are made of them. Self-medication, such as use of alcohol and other mind-altering drugs is common.

These children are the least understood of all the groups that exhibit atypical behaviors. Often they are seen as troublemakers because their parents and teachers do not understand or acknowledge the serious nature of their psychiatric conditions. Treatments include (1) supervised use of psychotropic medications, (2) individual, peer group and family counseling, and (3) behavior management. Hospitalization often is beneficial because it permits a more in-depth analysis of behaviors, moods, thought patterns and reactions to specific medications.

Pervasive Developmental Disabilities

There are a number of physical and medical conditions that interfere with normal learning and development. The more severe developmental disabilities reflect significant neurological abnormalities. Most common amongst these are mental retardation, autism, and cerebral palsy.

Most children who suffer from these developmental disabilities are identified early in life because they do not exhibit normal physical, cognitive and/or social development. They are under the care of specialists long before they reach school age. They require specialized education and training. Few achieve independence as adults.

Psychiatric Conditions

Children with medically significant psychiatric illnesses probably are the most feared and least understood of all groups exhibiting atypical behaviors. Frequently these children are also classified as troublemakers. Parents, teachers, and peers are unable to grasp the seriousness of their condition. Accurate diagnoses are essential to the identification of effective interventions. Possible treatments typically require the use of psychotropic medications as well as behavior modification, environmental alterations and counseling. Goals of these interventions include:

- Stabilization of moods.

- Reduction of psychotic ideation.

- Facilitation of improved cognitive and social functioning.

Social and Cultural Factors

All groups of people have a hierarchy of social and behavioral expectations and roles as their members move from one stage of life to the next. Most parents accept their responsibilities to foster social development in their children. They understand the role of parenting typically spans several life stages. Most adults also realize that expectations within each of these stages vary according to the child's physical, cognitive-intellectual, social, spiritual and emotional development. Thus, while all parents expect to foster social adaptation in their child or children, the specific demands of that task are quite different for parents of a pre-school child compared to one in high school.

Piaget's extensive observations and analysis of children's behaviors identified distinct changes in their thinking and problem-solving as they mature. In normal children, there is a transition from literal, concrete and simplistic views of personal and social events to sophisticated reasoning and analysis. This permits increasingly astute examination of experiences and a capacity to generate effective responses. Thus, over time children's abilities to reason, judge and problem-solve increasingly approximate that of mature adults.

The understanding and application of Piaget's Theories allow us to communicate more effectively with children: we can set valid expectations, present information, and guide children in a format readily useable to them. Integration of these data with knowledge of physical and cultural differences facilitates optimal cognitive and social-emotional development.

Gender Role Behaviors

Gender differences are apparent in the behaviors of pre-school children. Some of these differences are rooted in their genetic make-up. They reflect society's beliefs and attitudes about parenting. As a group, pre-adolescent boys are encouraged to be more physically active, dominant, self-assertive and aggressive than are girls of comparable ages. Girls are expected to be more passive, but are also encouraged to be more emotionally sensitive, inter-related, submissive and nurturing. These learned attitudes and behaviors tend to persist throughout life. This is because they are encouraged and rewarded in pre-adolescent children, then subsequently reinforced by both maturation and the influence of social expectations. Thus, society both permits and rewards the most self-assertive dominance and aggression on the part of boys, as compared to girls.

Experiences mold the attitudes and behaviors of school-age children. Those who observe aggression in real life, on television or in movies are likely to incorporate similar behaviors into their own actions. The consequences of their experiences are two-fold:

> • First, children who view violence tend to incorporate it into their response repertoire. Those who view television programs and movies that promote aggression as an acceptable means of resolving conflicts and moral dilemmas tend to act in more aggressive ways than do children who have not acquired these images as a part of their behavioral repertoire.

> • Second, children who learn that violence is socially appropriate also expect to be victims.

Pre-adolescent children do not appreciate the incongruity of using violence in the pursuit of praiseworthy goals. As girls are increasingly allowed and actively encouraged to participate in sports, pursue studies and enter careers until recently open only to boys, they adopt attitudes and behaviors associated with a competitive spirit. However, male children are not routinely encouraged to value emotional sensitivities defined as being feminine. These include attitudes and social skills that promote tolerance, compassion and empathy. This somewhat rigid adherence to traditional, stereotypical definitions of acceptable male behaviors fosters a greater tolerance for aggression on the part of boys.

Physical Abnormalities

Many developmental abnormalities reflect "hard-wired" physical, mental, emotional and/or social disabilities. These are permanent. These are impediments to normal growth and development. Most include observable differences in physical, behavioral and social functioning. They differ with respect to both severity and visibility. Some are very apparent. Others require identification through extensive medical and/or psychological examinations. A partial list of *Physical Abnormalities* includes:

- Attention-deficit hyperactivity disorder.

- Learning and behavior disorders.

- Mental retardation.

- Conduct disorder.

- Autism.

- Cerebral palsy.

Psychiatric Conditions includes:

- Schizophrenia.

- Bipolar disorder.

- Generalized anxiety disorder.

- Obsessive-compulsive disorder.

With few exceptions, these physical conditions include permanent neurological, cognitive, physical, behavioral and/or social-emotional traits that preclude normal learning and behaviors. They require educational and behavioral interventions, medical and psychiatric treatments, medications, physical and occupational therapies, and specialized vocational training.

Physical Disabilities

These neurological abnormalities effect social development, behavior, and learning. These disabilities also cause the affected children to behave differently from their peers.

This often limits their exposure to, and participation in, age-appropriate activities that are critical for normal child development. Therefore, these handicapping conditions constitute impediments that become increasingly significant with age. Thus, a violent adolescent is likely to have exhibited maladaptive behaviors and ideas long before he/she engages in the kind of violent acts that harm self and others.

Public efforts to address violence in this country have been largely futile. Exceptions are programs to promote an integrated and cohesive community effort to coordinate the efforts of education, law enforcement, churches and other community service agencies in intervention programs at a neighborhood level. Violence in schools has increased dramatically in recent years. Children are exhibiting aggressive behaviors at younger ages than were typical in the past. Factors that have been cited as contributions to aggression in schools include those common to the society at large.

SCHOOL VIOLENCE: A SOCIAL VIEWPOINT

Cultural Factors:

- Images defining masculinity in terms of aggressive behavior.

- Excessive glorification of contact sports.

- Depiction of violence in visual media (TV, videotapes, compute games and movies); aggression as a learned means of gaining advantage over others.

- Need for, and hope of gaining peer acceptance.

- Availability of weapons.

- Lack of effective adult supervision.

- Absence of meaningful, extended family supports.

- Limited opportunities for meaningful work for adolescent males.

- High incidence of single-parent families (mostly mothers).

- Unavailability of positive male role models.

- Emphasis on treatment, rather than prevention.

- Lack of, and/or ineffective psychiatric treatment.

- Ineffective social, legal and psychiatric interventions.

- Lack of parental involvement in their children's education.

- Poor communication and cooperation between parents and educators.

- Limited involvement by community entities such as churches and civic organizations.

- Dynamics of peer groups.

- Increased rates of social change.

- Availability of opiates, barbiturates, benzodiazepine, etc.

- Instructional emphasis on verbal skills.

- Limited opportunities for learning and application of nonverbal skills.

- Reliance on lectures and reading as primary means of information dissemination.

- Excessively large class sizes.

- Limited resources.

- Lack of sufficient administrative support for teachers.

Physical-Psychiatric Disorder

Prenatal Exposure to Toxic Substances: These include the effects of maternal drug and alcohol abuse as well as vicarious exposure to environmental toxins such as heavy metals, pesticides, residue of prescription and over-the-counter drugs in water, and other unidentified sources.

Subtle Neurological Abnormalities and their Causes Include:

- Family genetic patterns.
- Mutations of existing genes.
- Prenatal infections.
- Poor maternal nutrition.
- Post-natal physical neglect and abuse.
- Lack of age-appropriate mental stimulation.
- Social isolation.
- Subtle neurological abnormalities.
- Lowered intelligence.
- Poor verbal abilities that foster acting out to communicate.

Undiagnosed Neurological Disorders that Trigger Behavioral Outbursts:

- Prenatal exposure to toxic substances.
- Subtle neurological abnormalities.
- Lowered intelligence.
- Poor verbal abilities that foster communicating by acting out.

- Undiagnosed neurological disorders that trigger behavioral outbursts.

Family Abuse or Neglect:

- Subtle changes in neurological functioning.
- Increased prevalence of psychiatric disorder.
- Increased risk of depression.

Psychiatric Disorders (Depression):

- Disturbances in appetite.
- Sleep disturbances.
- Low energy, chronic fatigue.
- Low self-esteem.
- Poor concentration; difficulty making decisions.
- Irritability.
- Aggression.
- Chronic anxiety.
- Excessive, irrational, unwarranted fears.
- Somatic discomforts such as chest pain, stomach aches, and headaches.
- Hyper-vigilance.
- School violence.

- Hypochondria's.
- Restlessness.
- Difficulty with concentration.
- Muscle tension.
- Sleep disturbances.

Inattention:

- Failure to pay close attention to details.
- Makes careless mistakes.
- Does not seem to listen often.
- Often does not follow through on instructions.
- Easily distracted by extraneous stimuli.
- Disorganized.
- Often loses items necessary for activities.
- Fails to complete assignments.
- Often forgetful during daily activities.
- Hyperactive.
- Fidgets, squirms in seat, leaves seat, often runs about or climbs excessively.
- Often has difficulty engaging in quiet leisure activities.
- "On the go" at all times.

- Impulsivity: often blurts out answers before questions are completed.

- Has difficulty waiting for their turn.

- Interrupts or intrudes upon others.

Conduct Disorder:

- Is aggressive towards people and animals.

- Lies, fights, threatens, and intimidates others.

- Used a weapon that can cause serious physical harm to others.

- Has been physically cruel to people.

- Often initiates physical fights.

- Has stolen while confronting a victim.

- Forces someone into sexual activity.

- Destroys property.

- Deliberately engaged in setting fires with the intention of causing serious damage.

- Deliberately destroyed the property of others by various means.

- Deceitful.

- Steals.

Psychiatric Disorders:

- Has broken into someone' else's house, building or car.

- Often lies to obtain goods or favors or to avoid obligations.

- Has stolen items of non-trivial value without confronting a victim.

- Has been guilty of serious violations of rules.

- Often stays out nights despite parental prohibitions, beginning before age thirteen.

- Ran away from home overnight at least twice while living at a parent's or parental surrogate's home.

- Often truant from school, beginning before age thirteen.

Oppositional Defiant Disorder:

- A pattern of negativistic, hostile, and/or defiant behavior lasting for at least six months.

- Loses temper often.

- Often argues with adults.

- Often actively defies or refuses to comply with adults' requests or rules.

- Deliberately annoys people often.

- Often blames others for his/her mistakes.

- Is often touchy or easily annoyed by others.

- Often angry and resentful.

- Often spiteful or vindictive.

Intermittent Explosive Disorder:

- Unstable moods along with aggressive behaviors.

- Several discrete episodes of failure to resist aggressive impulses, resulting in serious aggressive acts or property destruction.

- The degree of aggressiveness expressed is grossly out of proportion to any precipitating psychosocial stressors.

Learning Disabilities:

- Difficulty acquiring reading, math, spelling and/or written language expression.

- Delays in developmental coordination skills.

- Attention and concentration difficulties significantly greater than would be predicted based upon the student's intelligence and educational experience.

- Often lead to under-achievement; social stigma, frustration and behavioral problems. May coexist with one or a combination of the psychiatric conditions noted previously.

Unidentifed, Untreated Neurological Disorders

Use of recreational drugs and the inappropriate use of prescribed drugs can be the proximate cause for aggressive behaviors. We tend to focus on this use and underestimate other factors that cause students to be vulnerable to the use of mind-altering substances. We also underestimate the extent to which mood-altering drugs are used to self-medicate.

Notes

Chapter Six

Effective Management of School Violence Prevention

BEHAVIOR MANAGEMENT

This form of management can be accomplished by developing system-wide, anti-violence policies that are taught *and* implemented at *all* instructional levels.

A key first step is to identify potential aggressors. Many of them will be males with average to low-average intelligence, exhibiting limited academic interests and skills. These students typically are action-oriented males who may begin with threats of aggression. They then quickly move on to taking action if their intimidations are not immediately successful **(see Behavior/Conduct Disorders)**.

However, a minority of aggressive students may have very good social skills. These are verbal and manipulative. These aggressors begin with threats and intimidation, and next move to physical aggression if necessary **(see Sociopathic Personality Traits)**.

Aggressive females tend to be verbal, but less physically aggressive. Following are some *Intervention Techniques* to consider at this Behavior Management Stage.

Interventions:

- Establish a classroom environment that minimizes the potential for violence.

- Clearly define rules and expectations.

- Define logical consequences for rule violations.

- Use reminders and warnings effectively.

- Establish a Zero Tolerance for dangerous behaviors with fairly enforced standards.

- Accept all students, but not their inappropriate behaviors.

- Give positive attention to all students.

- Implement educational, rather than punitive attitudes.

- Give students responsibilities regarding appropriate school behaviors.

- Tell students what to do, rather than what not to do.

- Be specific. Be generous with praise for acceptable behaviors.

- Begin early: at the preschool, kindergarten and elementary school level.

- Teach these management skills to parents, to enhance out-of-school behaviors, and to support your in-class efforts.

- Involve students and parents as active participants.

- Teach conflict resolution and mediation.

- Offer students equally acceptable alternatives, whenever possible.

- Teach students at their actual instructional levels.

- Identify both potential victims and aggressors.

- Develop intervention plans to target both individuals and groups.

- Teach group dynamics.

- Understand: the aggressive student at school may be the victim at home, or in a different setting.

- Teach potential victims to be more appropriately assertive.

- Teach verbal communication skills.

- Have well-defined back-up systems in place, say – a Buddy-Teacher System.

- **DO NOT** engage in physical altercations with students.

- In a crisis, maintain a safe distance.

- Do not use provocative language.

- Have security officer(s) in place – visible within the school – and immediately available.

- Develop procedures that allow teachers and administrators to share documented information regarding students' behavior. Do this in a manner that promotes safety and encourages students to report problematic events.

- Document problematic behaviors and incidents.

- Promote optimal growth in all areas of normal development.

- Understand: no child will be exactly on-track in all growth areas at any give time.

- Be both tolerant and understanding. View "problems" as opportunities for teaching your child and enhancing your relationship with him/her.

- Know your child's friends, their parents, teachers, coach and all others who have a significant influence in his/her life. Cooperate with these adults in promoting age-appropriate attitudes, values and behaviors.

Medical Interventions:

- Medications.

- Outpatient Psychiatric Treatment.

- Inpatient Psychiatric Treatment.

- Residential Placement.

A CASE STUDY APPROACH

Case Studies offer a slice-of-life reality to any field of study or research. The following three mini cases give you:

- A brief glimpse into the real world of child behavior within a hostile environment; and

- A chance to weigh the positive and negative dynamics at work in each of these mini-cases.

Identify in each of the following case studies:

- The approximate developmental age of the child/adolescent;

- How the child's actual behaviors reflect these developmental levels; and

- The ways in which lags in reaching developmental norms contributed to the child's thinking and actions.

- *Identify* both obvious and possible parenting failures as being factors that contributed to and/or worsened the child's behavior problems.

- *Identify* failures by community agencies and resources that left these children vulnerable at ages where they lacked the maturity to cope with the issues that confronted them.

Mini-Case One –
Thirteen-year-old Bobby and his Pawn Shop Heist

Bobby is a thirteen-year-old boy who lives with his biological mother. They live in an apartment in an economically depressed area. His mother works long hours. He has no contact with his father.

Bobby is supposed to be in school, but he dislikes school. Often he hides in an unlocked apartment. After school, he hangs out with a group of boys of similar age who live in his neighborhood. One day they all decide to "look around" in a nearby pawnshop. Each of them sees items they want. Later, they discuss plans to rob the store. One boy has access to a gun.

The following morning, the gang enters the shop. Bobby points the gun at the owner. Each boy then takes the item he wants. They leave. The store's owner calls the police. When they arrive, they begin to search the vacant apartment complex. They find Bobby in the abandoned apartment with the fishing pole he stole from the shop. He is arrested and placed in the juvenile pod of the local jail.

The prosecuting attorney requests that Bobby be tried as an adult. Psychological testing indicates he has an IQ in the 60 to 69 range. Thus, Bobby is mentally retarded. Despite this finding, Bobby is certified as an adult and convicted. He is placed in a prison unit with other adolescents. When he is 18, Bobby will be certified as an adult and transferred to an adult prison.

**Mini-Case Two –
Rita at 16: Molested, Unwed Mother, Murderer**

Rita is 16, the eldest of two brothers and two sisters. Both parents work. At about age four, her father began to sexually molest her when her mother was not home. Eventually, this activity included intercourse. When Rita reported this to her teacher, her father was arrested. Eventually he reached a plea arrangement in which he agreed to individual and family counseling. After his counseling was completed, all charges were dropped, the court records sealed, and he was allowed to return home.

His sexual abuse of Rita continued until she was 13. At that time, she ran away from home and began to live on the streets with other adolescents. She worked at odd jobs. She became sexually active with one of the gang members, and got pregnant. When Rita's daughter was born, her parents applied for (and obtained) custody of the child.

One night, Rita and her friends attempted to rob a group of homeless people. They resisted. A fight broke out. A homeless person was shot and killed. She was charged with murder. Her defense attorney was granted his request for a psychological examination. Rita told the story of her abused childhood. Her story was verified by her attorney through his access to her sealed court records. However, he could not use them as part of her defense.

**Mini-Case Three –
A Gang Murder; Fred Guilty by Association**

Fred is 15. He came to New Mexico from Illinois to live with his maternal grandmother. His mom feared for his safety in Illinois because she worked long hours and they lived in a rough part of town. Soon after Fred arrived at his New Mexico high school, older boys began to pressure him to join their gang.

Fred didn't want to do this, but felt intimidated and had no other friends to support him. When a man was murdered by one of his gang's members, Fred was blamed. Because he had a gang tattoo on his hand, the police believed he was guilty of the murder. They came to his grandmother's house where he was sleeping on the couch. The police fired canisters into the house that gave off toxic fumes. Every window in the house was broken.

Fred was confined to the juvenile pod of the local county jail. He was held there for about four months before he was scheduled for trial. During that time, he was threatened and harassed by the older, more aggressive inmates.

PART III

Bloodborne Pathogens (BBP) and Related Safety Issues

It is beyond the scope of this work to define and examine all the causal factors that contribute to this world of violence we live in. However, it is essential to consider some of the broader forces involved in order to apply current methods of violence problem identification and control in our schools.

Almost all societies struggle to resolve the conflict between the need for social structure and order, and the individual rights of their citizens. Or put another way, individuals must decide how much personal liberty they will sacrifice to maintain the benefits of an orderly structure in which they can interact and function.

Measures such as the Homeland Security legislation (although generally accepted as necessary for the greater good of us all), have raised serious questions regarding the core issue of the balance between individual rights and the need for the preservation and protection of our society.

Before we discuss specific hazard-protection concepts, it is necessary to restate two basic concepts (or assumptions) unique to the scholastic workplace. Although the basic measures traditionally used to protect people, products and facilities apply, it is still very important to remember this:

1. School personnel in general have not received a specifically high priority for receiving protection.

2. Schools have not been considered as a source of wealth that deserves protection as much as any other valuable resource of our nation.

With minimal changes, the Loss Prevention/Business Interruption principles used in industry can also be applied to scholastic work sites. Traditionally, the hazards of fire, severe weather, and other natural occurrences have been recognized and addressed in schools. Some commonly shared dangers include:

• **Intruders from outside the facility** — Persons who commit acts of burglary, robbery and vandalism, who are violating restraint orders, who seek revenge (a terminated employee).

• **Persons whose presence in the facility is normal** – Who suddenly and unexpectedly commit acts of violence.

Defenses against such traumas include: (1) Formal written polices that address such occurrences, (2) Physical barriers, entry control and related structural elements, and (3) Pre-arranged agreements with local law enforcement authorities.

Recently, "internal assembly" within the physical structure (vs. evacuation) has been expanded to include situations involving release of hazardous chemicals, or other hazards involving rapid or catastrophic occurrences. In schools with mostly younger children, it is "presumed" that directing and controlling orderly movement to assembly areas is a relatively simple matter.

With older children and teen-agers, frequent drills, educating about the nature and effect of chemical and biological agents, and involvement of students in pre-planning under trained supervision may all make "Shelter in Place" more effective. School stakeholders should insist on drills and exercises being held frequently enough to ensure everyone knows how to respond when necessary.

Unity brings strength. While the individual may be frightened, inadequate, or ill-equipped to deal with the multiple threats we now face, individuals with a common cause can join together to address these issues, with a collective strength greater than the sum of the individuals involved emerging.

Notes

Chapter Seven

Diseases Contracted from BBP and Required Protective Measures

---

*You and your teaching co-workers have received limited information and instruction about illnesses resulting from exposure to Bloodborne Pathogens (BBP). Until now, this issue seemed alien; not related to your profession. But this morning, a school teacher-colleague stated that he was **very** concerned about the possible consequences of a wound he sustained while separating two brawling students.*

Both students were bleeding from their cuts. He believes some of the blood may have gotten into his wound. When he reported this to the principal, he received vague feedback about performing some self-treatment. He received no encouragement to seek medical treatment and surveillance.

In fact, it was made clear to him that seeking medical care would "create a lot of paperwork" and adverse comments about the school's safety record and worker's comp experience. You and your colleagues agree that protection and assistance must be available under federal or state law, but you are unsure how to get that assistance. **What action can you take to solve this problem?**

Key Concepts and Data in This Chapter

1. Bloodborne Pathogens (BBP) as a source of danger to teachers and other scholastic employees.

2. A definition of Bloodborne Pathogens.

3. Consequences of exposure to human bodily fluids.

4. Avenues of exposure to BBP.

5. Employee protective methods.

Bloodborne Pathogens (BBP) as a Source of Danger to Teachers and other Scholastic Employees

Understandably, teachers and other educational facility employees are concerned about the immediate results of direct physical assaults on them by students, or during their attempts to prevent or stop physical assaults between students. Physical trauma such as bruises, fractured bones, damaged teeth, visual impairment and other direct and immediate injury to the body are an unfortunate fact of life in schools from the elementary level through high school. Student injuries are the subject of much discussion – while scholastic workplace injuries to workers receive relatively little attention.

Unfortunately, the immediate physical consequences of such conflicts may be only the first phase of injury or illness arising from violent acts in the academic workplace. As in every area of workplace activity, long-term disability or even death may result from physical injuries received from exposure to individuals suffering from certain diseases involving fluid circulation systems of their bodies.

Although considerable attention has been given to this potential disease exposure in the industrial workplace, little proportionate attention has been directed to scholastic workplace employees. There appear to be a number of reasons for this situation:

1. There has been limited perception of teachers and other educational system employees as being exposed to frequent physical violence. Outside of widely publicized incidents such as those involving firearms or multiple murders, little has been reported in the media. And in these instances, the greatest focus and concern has been placed on student exposure to harm, rather then the dangers to school personnel.

2. The common public perception is that the education workplace presents little exposure to the hazards encountered in the industrial workplace, including physical violence. Indeed, even many educational institution personnel do not recognize the hazards of workplace violence that their environment exposes them to on a daily basis.

3. Certain "gaps" or gray areas of safety responsibility and jurisdiction tend to exclude public educational institution employees from the protections commonly guaranteed by federal or state legislation to workers in other areas.

4. School Boards (which tend to be extremely conservative) have been reluctant to address the entire topic of workplace violence and it's consequences involving disease. Even in progressive school districts, employee training is frequently very simplistic. Protective equipment and immediate care arrangements are limited, and the legal rights of teachers and other school employees are rarely addressed or defined.

5. Unions which represent teachers and other academic institution employees have concentrated their

efforts on improving wages and traditional benefits, with little attention to this health area of concern.

A Definition of Bloodborne Pathogens (BBP)

This is a good place to define and discuss BBP. Widespread attention has been given to the nature and significance of BBPs and the diseases they cause. Both legislation and regulations for the protection of the general public and many classes of employees have been developed. It is our hope that discussions within this book will assist in the development of protective measures for public school employees as well.

Subpart Z - Toxic and Hazardous Substances of the Occupational Safety and Health Act, 29CFR1919.1 030 Bloodborne Pathogens contains the following definition of Bloodborne Pathogens in the text of the Standard: *"Pathogenic microorganisms that are present in human blood and can cause disease in humans. These pathogens include, but are not limited to, Hepatitis B virus (HBV) and human immunodeficiency virus (HIV)."* (1-1)

In addition, within the same Section of the federal standard, there is a related definition of potential Infectious Materials as well as blood which may expose humans to infection. According to the standard, *Other Potentially Infectious Materials* means:

    1. "The following human body fluids: semen, vaginal secretions, cerebrospinal fluid, synovial fluid, pleural fluid, pericardial fluid, peritoneal fluid, amniotic fluid, saliva in dental procedures, any body fluid that is visibly contaminated with blood, and all body fluids in situations where it is difficult or impossible to differentiate between body fluids;

    2. "Any unfixed tissue or organ (other than intact skin) from a human (living or dead); and

3. "HIV-containing cell or tissue cultures, organ cultures, and HIV or HBV-containing culture medium or other solutions; and blood, organs, or other tissues from experimental animals infected with HIV or HBV." (1-2 *ibid*).

It should be noted that in addition to saliva "in dental procedures," exposure to saliva from human bites is considered a potential exposure to disease from Bloodborne Pathogens. *Note* the definition: "*Parenteral* means *piercing mucous membranes or the skin barrier through such events as needle sticks, human bites, cuts or abrasions.*" (1-3 *ibid*) (emphasis added by author).

Consequences of Exposure to Human Bodily Fluids

For many years teachers and other educational institution employees have recognized and accepted the fact that working with groups of students exposed them to various infectious diseases. All the range of diseases associated with childhood (measles, mumps, whooping cough, etc.) as well as infestations such as lice, mites, etc. have been more or less accepted as a form of "occupational hazard."

At the same time, the potential for bodily injury arising from physical fighting, scuffling, wrestling, etc. among students has also been accepted as a part of workplace hazards. As mentioned earlier, it has been rare for such episodes to have been formally recognized by teachers, administrative personnel or support staff members as deserving or needing special attention beyond providing basic first aid care to injured parties. Concurrent disciplinary action has been directed toward isolation or expulsion of offenders on a case-by-case basis.

Today, the "traditional" secondary hazards of infection arising from bites, scratches, abrasions, etc. are recognized to be significantly increased by the possibility of contracting diseases which are either difficult or impossible to treat successfully. Given the range of diseases involved, it is critical that potential exposure to the body fluids of others be minimized. In addition, effective methods *must* be in place for responding promptly and effectively to minimize the consequences of this exposure.

UNIVERSAL PRECAUTIONS

A primary element of the federal OSHA Bloodborne Pathogens Standard is emphasis on the concept of *Universal Precautions*. This concept involves acceptance of the fact that exposure to *ANY* human bodily fluid should be considered a direct and actual source of infection with any of a wide range of diseases. Consequently, it is vital for people to:

- Shield themselves from such exposure(s) as much as possible.

- Wash any area of the body that comes in contact with such fluids thoroughly with soap and water, or other appropriate disinfectant agents.

- Remove, containerize and wash, or decontaminate prior to further use, or properly dispose of any exposed clothing or personal effects as a Biohazard.

Obviously, such procedures can only be followed if an appropriate facility equipped with necessary materials and supplies is readily available to those who need them. Specific requirements for optimizing the availability and effectiveness of elements needed to achieve Universal Precautions as set forth in the federal Bloodborne Pathogens Standard are presented.

However, a basic principle of self-protection is consistent emphasis on the washing of any part of the body exposed to the bodily fluids of others. The old maxim *"Clean hands don't spread germs"* is more true than ever. The precaution of washing your hands before eating, drinking, smoking, etc., **greatly** reduces the potential for infection. Also, every conscious effort should be made to avoid touching one's eyes or mouth after touching potentially contaminated materials prior to washing the hands .

Avenues of Exposure to BBP

ANY exposure to the bodily fluids of others can potentially result in transfer of Bloodborne Pathogens. Consequently, it is conceivable that so simple an act as touching an infected person who is sweating heavily, and then wiping the affected hand across one's mouth could result in an active transfer of the disease.

However, the likelihood of such a transfer is very limited. A similar potential exists if a person with an unhealed cut comes into direct contact with a bodily fluid from an infected person, which enters the area of the cut. Because of the irreversible effects of contracting a disease such as HIV, there is a tendency to be aggressively reluctant to come in contact with anyone known or suspected to be infected with any disease, or a person who is a stranger. However, with proper training and equipment, physical interaction with potentially infected people may be undertaken with greatly reduced chances of contacting a Bloodborne Pathogen disease.

Although there is a limited exposure potential for infection from airborne particles dispersed by coughing or other similar, relatively dispersed bodily fluids, the greatest danger arises from *direct exposure* to concentrated bodily fluids. Optimum protection can be achieved by:

- Keeping the Universal Precautions doctrine in mind.

- Using personal protective equipment (gloves, mask, disposable clothing, etc.) when dealing with anyone whenever a potential for transferring bodily fluids exists.

- Washing exposed body areas, clothing and effects immediately after exposure.

- Being careful when handling an object that could be considered a *"sharp,"* (i.e. broken glass, hypodermic needles, etc.), not handling such objects with bare hands, disposing of protective gloves immediately after proper disposal of the item, and washing your hands thoroughly after removing and disposing of the protective gloves.

- Consulting with a physician or other health care professional to gain a clear understanding of the specific hazards you face, and how to best protect yourself.

Employee Protective Methods

There are certain accepted methods for ensuring employee protection. Under the federal standard and those of federal OSHA-approved state plans, employers are required to provide an effective protection program. Since the nature and extent of exposure in each workplace area is different, the employer is required to develop an *Exposure Control Plan* that identifies potential BBP exposure hazards, and provides appropriate facilities, equipment, and training for employee protection.

Exposure Control Plan

Each worksite subject to federal or state occupational safety and health administration authority must have a **written** Exposure Control Plan. The Plan must have a minimum of three (3) basic elements:

1. Exposure Determination:

A listing by job classification of those workplace jobs that involve the following degrees of exposure to BBP:

- All employees in this job have potential exposure to BBP.

- Some employees in this job have potential exposure to BBP.

- A list of tasks, procedures, or groups of closely related tasks and procedures in which potential exposure to BBP occurs.

(**NOTE:** Jobs/tasks must be listed without regard to protection by Personal Protective Equipment provided).

2. A Schedule and Method for Establishing:

- Methods of compliance.

- Designated medical laboratory facilities for testing for HIV and HBV presence in fluid samples from exposed employees.

- HBV vaccination and post-exposure evaluation and follow-up.

- Communication of hazards to employees.

- Record keeping for data related to this program.

3. <u>Procedure for Evaluation of Circumstances Surrounding Exposure Incidents (Hepatitis B Vaccination and Post-Exposure Evaluation and Follow-Up):</u>

Engineering and Work Practice Controls

First – To ensure compliance with the comprehensive approach to employee protection established within the standards of the federal OSHAct, employers are required to utilize three interacting protection methodologies: *First – Engineering Controls* designed, installed and maintained to minimize exposure to hazards. *Second* – These are to be supplemented by *Administrative Controls* designed to prevent exposure to hazardous substances above minimum levels. *Third – Personal Protective Equipment* (PPE) is to be used by individual employees to minimize exposure to hazardous substances not completely screened out by engineering and administrative means. PPE may *NOT* be used as a substitute for engineering and administrative controls.

Second – However, it is apparent that in the academic workplace, relatively few engineering or administrative controls are practical. Possible exceptions are industrial shop classroom facilities, and of course, school maintenance and repair facilities (storage and distribution equipment for grounds care and maintenance, etc.). Cafeteria food handling facilities should also contain certain applicable control systems such as ventilation systems, food preparation equipment guards, and related safety and health equipment that enhance protection against exposure to Bloodborne Pathogens.

In addition, laboratory facilities devoted to chemical experimentation, physics studies and related equipment and materials storage facilities should have appropriate specific control programs in place. Protection from BBP should be one of these programs.

Third – The required facilities for washing and

disinfecting represent *Engineering Controls,* as do provisions for containment facilities and equipment for contaminated clothing and other items. Provision and enforcement of procedures for dealing with exposure to BBP or the release of such substances constitute *Administrative Controls.* Because of considerable use of PPE in the scholastic workplace, let's briefly discuss this equipment.

Personal Protective Equipment (PPE)

PPE is defined in the federal OSHA Standard as *"Specialized clothing or equipment worn by an employee for protection against a hazard. General work clothes (e.g. uniforms, pants, shirts, or blouses) not intended to function as protection against a hazard are not considered to be personal protective equipment."* (1- 4 *ibid*).

Remember: such equipment is to be provided by the employer as a supplement to comprehensive *Engineering Controls,* or *Administrative Controls,* or a combination of the two. Essentially, use of PPE is looked upon as a way of maximizing the combined effectiveness of methods used to protect employees.

With employment areas under the jurisdiction and administration of federal and state safety and health management departments, employers must provide a written program outlining the following:

- The specific types of PPE to be used.

- Documented employee training provided by a qualified entity as to how it is to be donned, doffed, cared for, or disposed of after use.

- Where the PPE is to be stored when not in use, what maintenance and repair measures are in place, and where on-site they are located.

- Who is authorized and equipped to repair the PPE.

- Who is responsible for issuing PPE, providing appropriate training in caring for it, and usage as well as proper storage, plus disposal methods and facilities.

- Requirements that work area supervisors ensure that PPE is used and disposed of as set forth in work area rules and procedures.

Limitations of PPE

PPE should be selected on the basis of suitability, durability, frequency and extent of use, and availability when needed. User personnel must be fully trained and understand the relative strength and degree of protection provided by the PPE. Example: vinyl or latex gloves are not always suitable for collecting broken glass, cracked test tubes, or hypodermic needles. Most one-time use/disposable protective clothing provides limited protection against penetration by significant quantities of bodily fluids. Suitable wash-down/shower facilities should be provided for personnel who are potentially exposed to significant quantities of bodily fluids. Employees are required to follow all rules governing the use of PPE, give the equipment proper care and use, and report any PPE damage or defects to the designated supervision.

There are definite limitations to the nature and extent of protection provided by PPE. Variables such as the severity and duration of exposure to hazard(s), the type of PPE involved, its designated capabilities, and other site-specific issues need to be clearly and completely understood by the person relying on PPE for any portion of personal protection. With these considerations in mind, the role of PPE in protection against BBP in the scholastic workplace follows this profile:

Eye Protection – When the possibility exists of blood or other bodily fluids being splashed into the eyes of a person, that person should be equipped with suitable eye protection in the form of glasses configured to minimize the possibility of the bodily fluid entering the eyes. A dependable, readily available source of fresh, unadulterated water sufficient to allow a minimum of 15 minutes of continuous flushing of the eyes should be available to ensure thorough flushing of the eyes.

Face Protection – To protect against ingestion of bodily fluids through the mouth, or inspiration of bodily fluids through the nose into the lungs, a suitable face mask should be available. A disposable fiber mask of suitable density with tie-strings or over-the-ear sidepieces should be appropriate for all non-medical care duties.

Hand Protection – Disposable vinyl or latex gloves should be provided to all personnel exposed to bodily fluids arising from touching individuals who are bleeding, sweating, eliminating, crying, spitting or otherwise releasing bodily fluids. Individuals who are required to handle or dispose of human or animal waste or related organic materials should be provided with appropriate, specific training and necessary tools and equipment.

Protective Clothing – Disposable or washable clothing such as smocks, jacket/pant suits, or aprons should be available for the use of all personnel expected to have exposure to bodily fluids in the course of their work. Shoe covers and washable footwear shall be provided for those required to handle or clean-up waste containing bodily fluids.

Notes

Chapter Eight

Regulatory Protection Against BBP Diseases for School Workplace Employees

---

Your school is located in a large U.S. city. Like all Americans, you were appalled by the destruction of the Murrah Building in Oklahoma City, and the attack on the World Trade Center in New York. Although there have been no specific threats of such attacks on your city, you still have a nagging feeling of dread about your safety and that of your students, family and friends. So far, the only information or training you have received from school authorities has been very general and vague — not what you consider to be applicable to your classroom and school workplace.

You ask yourself: "What am I expected to do if an act of terrorism or an emergency occurs close enough to my school to affect me and those around me?" Where do you get practical, usable information to prepare for such an event and use it? What specific steps should you and your colleagues take during an emergency to protect the lives of your students – and yourself?

It was The Big Game for Upton Central. Win this one and it was off to the state championship game at the university. On the kick-off, the helmet of Upton's league-leading rusher got ripped off and he took a severe elbow shot to the nose. Screaming with pain, blood gushing from his nostrils, he staggered to the sidelines and collapsed into his coach's arms.

Coach's indoctrination about BBP was fresh in his mind, and he instinctively avoided the injured player's outstretched arms. This didn't sit too well with the hyped-up crowd, hungry for a victory at any price. Scattered boos drifted down from the bleachers.

The trainer, complete with a PPE medical kit, was better prepared to handle such emergencies and began to treat the player. Coach kept the injured player out of the game – the bleeding wouldn't stop completely. The opposing team scored two quick touchdowns and suddenly things weren't looking too good for Upton. The crowd began a thunderous chant to put the star player back into the game, but Coach wasn't taking any chances and kept him on the bench. **Was Coach overreacting to the blood danger? What was his responsibility to the well-being of the player?**

Key Concepts and Data in This Chapter

Protection for Teachers and School Workplace Employees Provided by:

1. 1970 Williams-Steiger Occupational Safety and Health Act.

2. State Occupational Safety and Health Legislation.

3. Local and Public Agencies.

4. School Districts, Boards, Administrative Authorities and Unions.

PROTECTION PROVIDED BY THE
1970 WILLIAMS-STEIGER ACT

The 1970 Williams-Steiger Occupational Safety and Health Act (commonly referred to as the OSHAct) became effective April 28, 1971. Its intention: "Assure so far as possible every working man and woman in the nation safe and healthful working conditions, and to preserve our human resources."

It would be reasonable to presume, given the broad language of this Purpose Statement, that scholastic workplace employees can look to the OSHAct for guaranteed protection of their health and safety, backed by the full weight of U.S. Federal Law. *In reality, employees of many public school systems do not have the benefit of this assured protection.*

Employees of private educational institutions are covered by the OSHAct. The status of their "employer" falls within the definitions of the Act. However, educational institutions operated by church organizations have some exemptions from coverage. Generally, people engaged in non-religious related activities (kitchen workers, bus drivers, custodial and maintenance workers, grounds-keeping personnel) *are* covered by the Act. And many classifications of teachers, teacher's aides, or instructors also are covered.

However, like public school employees, there may be exceptions and qualifiers that substitute state authority for federal authority. As we will see, access to federal OSHAct protection *is not* available to public school employees. This is due to the structure of the Act, which reflects the intent of Congress to carefully preserve the rights and entitlements of the states as set forth in the Constitution of the United States.

Section 29 CFR 1975.5 of the OSHAct contains definitions that separate public school employees from direct coverage under the Act. The following important explanations and definitions help clarify this situation.

Section 29 CFR 1975.5(a)

General Definition – The definition of the term *"Employer"* in Section 3 (5) of the Act excludes the United States, the 50 States, and political subdivisions of a State:

(5) Employer – A person engaged in a business affecting commerce who has employees, but does not include the United States or any State or political subdivision of a State.

(7) State – Defined in Section 3(7) of the Act includes a State of the United States, the District of Columbia, Puerto Rico, the Virgin Islands, American Samoa, Guam, and the Trust Territory of the Pacific Islands.

Since States, as defined in Section 3(7) of the Act and political subdivision thereof are not regarded as employers under Section 3(5) of the Act, they would not be covered as employers under the Act. *Exception:* Section 18(c)(6) and the pertinent regulations thereunder require as a condition of approval of a State Plan by the Secretary of Labor that such plan: (6) Contain(s) satisfactory assurances that such State will, to the extent permitted by its law, establish and maintain an effective and comprehensive occupational safety and health program applicable to all employees of public agencies of the State and its political subdivisions, which program is as effective as the standards contained in an approved plan. (OSHAct, 29 CFR 1975, - OSHAct of 1970, Section 18, 12/26/2003).

Remember: the OSHAct provides for States wanting to develop their own occupational safety and health legislation, and systems of administrative/enforcement and judicial review. Such programs are subject to review and approval by the U.S.

Department of Labor, Occupational Safety and Health Administration, under Section 18 of the federal OSHAct. States choosing to do so are responsible for enforcement of the approved plan. They may choose to collect fines and penalties for proven violations. In such States, public education facilities may be defined as an "employer."

The effect of this potential for fines and penalties is to create a strong inducement to school systems in such States to provide adequate BBP protection (and other protection programs) to their employees. However, even in Approved Plan States such as California, Wyoming, Washington, North Dakota, West Virginia, etc., schools are generally considered to be low hazard/low priority entities in relation to industrial firms. A list of States and territories with approved OSHAct Plans can be found in Appendix A.

Continuing with "what excludes public schools and their employees from protection under the federal OSHAct, Section 29 CFR 1975.5" (Coverage of Employees under the Williams-Steiger OSHA of 1970), certain tests are prescribed to establish applicability of the law. Entities are excluded as "Employers" subject to the following tests:

1975.5 (b)(1): "Any entity which has been created directly by the State, so as to constitute a department or administrative arm of the government or ...."

75.5 (b)(2): "Administered by individuals who are controlled by public officials and responsible to such officials or to the general electorate, shall be deemed to be a 'State or political subdivision thereof under Section 3(5) of the Act, and therefore not within the definition of employer, and consequently, not subject to the Act as an employer.' "

1975.5 (c): "Factors for Meeting the Tests. Various factors will be considered in determining whether an entity meets the tests discussed earlier. Some Factor examples are:

- Are the individuals who administer the entity appointed by a public official or elected by the general electorate?

- What are the terms and conditions of the appointment?

- Who may dismiss such individuals and under what procedures?

- What is the financial source of these individuals' salaries?

- Does the entity earn a profit?

- Are such profits treated as revenue?

- How are the entity's functions financed?

- What are the powers of the entity, and are they usually characteristic of a government rather than a private instrumentality (like the power of imminent domain?).

- How is the entity regarded under state and local law as well as under Federal laws?

- Is the entity exempted from state and local tax laws?

- Are the entity's bonds, if any, tax exempt?

- Are the entity's employees regarded like employees of other state and political subdivisions?

- What is the financial source of the employee payroll?

- How do employee fringe benefits, rights, obligations and restrictions of the entity's employees compare to those of the employees of other state and local departments and agencies?

In evaluating these Factors, due regard will be given to whether any occupational safety and health program exists to protect the entity's employees.

1975.5 (d): "eight of the Factors. The previous list of Factors is not exhaustive. No Factor, isolated from the particular facts of a case, is assigned any particular weight for the purpose of a determination by the Secretary of Labor as to whether a given entity is a 'State or political subdivision of a State' and as such, is not subject to the Act as an 'employer.' Each case must be viewed on its merits. Whether a single factor will be decisive, or whether the Factors must be viewed in their relationship to each other as part of a sum total, this also depends on the merits of each case."

1975.5 (e) (1) Entities normally not regarded as Employers under Section 3(5) of the OSHAct:

- ***State, County and Municipal Public Schools Boards & Commissions*** (Italics added by Author).

- State Department of Labor and Industry.

- State Highway and Motor Vehicle Department.

- State, County and Municipal Law Enforcement Agencies.

- Penal Institutions.

- State, County and Municipal Judicial Bodies.

- State University Boards of Trustees.

- Public Libraries.

Interesting: The issue of "incentives" for compliance represented by potential fines and penalties is a key factor in addressing the test questions raised in 1975.5 (c). In States subject to federal OSHA jurisdiction, the responsibility for providing safety and health protection is directed to the State. As noted previously, the State is expected to provide equal coverage, but frequently has no provision for fines and penalties itself. Provision is made for citations to be issued for alleged violations, but there is no provision for financial consequences. Public school workers in these jurisdictions are thus denied one of the strongest inducements for those who employ them to provide and maintain effective Bloodborne Pathogen and other forms of protection for related dangers.

To put this issue into perspective, a basic element of the philosophy upon which the OSHAct is based is the ***Theory of Unjust Enrichment.*** Here, all employers subject to the provisions of the Act are assumed to be in compliance until the U.S. DOL/OSHAdministration determines the employer is *NOT* in compliance, based on site inspections and other evaluation activity. Failure to identify and develop programs to gain compliance with regulatory standards subjects the employer to proposed fines and penalties as an inducement to stimulate compliance.

The presumption that failure to comply with the OSHAdministration's view of employer obligations gives OSHA the right to stipulate how money, time, and effort are to be spent to accomplish compliance has always been one of the primary objections to the OSHAct. Although many employers have always considered this government power to be unfairly intrusive, it was actually the final will of Congress. Also, no judicial challenge has succeeded in reversing this portion of the OSHAct.

In many of the States subject to Federal OSHA jurisdiction, the policy is for findings of apparent "Serious Violations" (as determined by the state agency) to be remanded for further investigation to the Federal OSHA's office having jurisdiction over that specific geographic area. However, a serious question exists:

"Can OSHA propose penalties or other sanctions for an entity outside its jurisdiction, such as a school board?"

From the foregoing it can be concluded that employees of public educational institutions are in an awkward position when seeking governmental protection from either federal or State-defined safety and health hazards, if their employer is located in a State under federal OSHA jurisdiction.

PROTECTION BY STATE OCCUPATIONAL SAFETY AND HEALTH LEGISLATION

Remember, there are twenty-six States and territories with approved OSHA equivalent plans in place. To maintain this autonomy, provisions of each plan must "equal or exceed" the requirements of the federal plan (OSHAct of 1970 - Sec. 18 - State Jurisdiction and State Plans).

In States subject to federal OSHA, legal mandates require the State entity responsible for worker safety and health to provide protection comparable to federal standards. However, lack of enforcement "teeth" in the form of fines and penalties may seriously weaken the responsible agency(s) from providing "real world" protection to employees whose employers are excluded from the federal definition of "employee." Let's now consider some aspects of protection provided by States with Federal OSHA Approved Plans.

Keep in mind that Congress was faced with a number of philosophical dilemmas that had to be resolved before the OSHAct could be passed into law. A primary issue was the extent to which the provisions of the act would apply to public entities. It is significant to note that Congress itself is excluded from the provisions of the OSHAct!

The U.S. Postal Service is subject to the Act as a result of specific legislation passed by Congress in 1998. Other divisions of the federal government are subject to compliance with equal obligations under programs of their own making and subsequent enforcement, or other parallel legislation governing such industries as railroads, aviation, trucking and shipping. The Department of Labor, Occupational Safety & Health Administration is mandated to assist where appropriate and when requested to do so by a specific agency.

State legislatures were faced with the difficult question of determining where the money for fines and penalties would come from when a non-profit colleague-agency was alleged to be noncompliant with safety regulation provisions. As noted previously, private industry has long been subject to such overhead expense considerations. However, how were agencies that draw revenues from public taxes for public services expected to generate revenues for such expenses? By its very nature, public services are those provided to benefit the entire society, and are expected to generate only sufficient revenue to pay their operating expenses. Quantifying the relative efficiency of a governmental agency in terms of accident cost control was a relatively new concept. Certainly, worker's compensation costs have been measured for years. Increases or decreases in the number and costs of accidents are a matter of record.

Yet, without such benchmarks as gross and net profit; costs of raw materials in relation to finished goods value, etc., public service entities are more difficult to measure and evaluate. Public schools, for example, can point only to population served expressed in annual number of graduates and various academic measurement methodologies.
Wear and tear/replacement cycles for fixed and consumable assets can be predicted based on experience, but accident costs are hard to quantify. In the same vein, other than mechanical and custodial operations, effective safety and health matters appear to be a relatively minor concern to school management. As discussed in earlier chapters, the

growing trend towards violence in the academic workplace has impacted this perception, but financial accommodation has been slow to follow.

Predictably, some States chose to include punitive inducements in the form of penalties and fines in their OSHA-approved plans, while others did not. It will be interesting to see how the issue of punishment for willful or criminal failure to comply with safety standards emerges in the public education arena. There is a growing trend to bring criminal action against individuals in private industry when they are perceived to be guilty of willful, wanton or deliberate violations of safety, health and environmental regulations.

U.S. DOL/OSHA cooperates officially with the U.S. Department of Justice in criminal proceedings under the Racketeering Influenced and Corrupt Organizations Act (RICO). And more recently, the Sarbanes-Oxley Act to perfect legal action against individual managers, officers and directors of firms in the private sector. It is unclear if the same vehicles may be used in the event of an episode in a governmental agency, or related function such as a public or private school where deaths or multiple serious injuries/illnesses occur, or are perceived to have been caused (even in part) by violations of safety standards and regulations.

The Department of Homeland Security will aggressively pursue action if either foreign or domestic terrorism is suspected in an occurrence involving death or multiple injuries or illnesses. They will rely on the interaction of both criminal and administrative departments to define and act where it is deemed necessary.

California has provisions for filing criminal charges for industrial/construction site fatalities or multiple serious injuries where willful or criminal negligence is suspected. Not only does CAL-OSHA have such powers to involve state law enforcement agencies in pursuing such actions. Most major California cities have designated law enforcement agencies at the city and county level dedicated to the investigation of industrial and construction accidents, and alleged intentional or willful violations of safety regulations.

Consideration of these matters may lead public school employees to despair of any meaningful support or protection from exposures to Bloodborne Pathogen-induced illnesses arising from incidents in the academic workplace. On balance, this is not the case. In every jurisdiction, whether under federal or state safety and health authority, **help is available.** It may not be as direct or clear cut as it is in other areas of employment, but powerful resources do exist.

Whether or not the authority has the power to propose fines, every State safety and health regulatory enforcement authority does have the power to issue citations for alleged failure of a public school to provide legally required protection against Bloodborne Pathogen-caused illness. The very issuance of such a citation can be a potent way to gain public awareness and support in gaining relief.

PROTECTION PROVIDED BY LOCAL AND PUBLIC AGENCIES

Help with pre-planning or responding to the consequences of injuries or illness from physical violence can be found with local (county or city) agencies that are extensions of (or complementary to) federal and state agencies. For example: the county and city health department, and police, fire, and ambulance departments can all be called upon for help.

Protection Provided by Other State Agencies

Because of growing concerns about Bloodborne Pathogen diseases, various other governmental agencies are initiating action for protecting the public and the individual. Public school employees may find supplemental support from other state entities such as a Health and Human Services Department, employee rights divisions of State Labor Departments, or other specific components of the state government. Certainly, all citizens have the right (and the power!) to contact elected representatives at both federal and State legislatures to request information, assistance and support. Non-governmental agencies such as the local United Fund Group has a variety of services available which can provide information, planning and response assistance.

PROTECTION PROVIDED BY SCHOOL DISTRICTS, BOARDS, ADMINISTRATIVE AUTHORITIES AND UNIONS

Many progressive public school systems have recognized the significant threat to the health and safety of their employees from violence in the scholastic workplace. Usually the primary emphasis has consistently been on the protection of students. However, real world factors such as worker's compensation claims, litigation, employee lost work time and other operational and financial aspects of the situation make it increasingly difficult for public school administration to side step or minimize the problem of workplace violence as it impacts their employees. Additionally, actual and potential liability from litigation is forcing formal recognition and action on these problems.

Response and Protection Programs are emerging in answer to scholastic violence concerns. Like any emerging methodology, they may have weak points, lapses, or omissions. The inherently conservative nature of academic enterprises works against bold or aggressive programs. However, school system administrators are generally recognizing that pre-planning is more effective and less burdensome than individual response to specific crisis incidents.

As noted earlier, the emergence of the federal Department of Homeland Security is serving to heighten violence awareness. Concrete action is being taken against violence in all its forms at all levels of our society. Part of this awareness will be progressively represented by availability of funds and resources to improve overall safety and health of all citizens.

Options for Public School Workplace Employees to Protect Themselves from Bloodborne Pathogen-Generated Diseases and other Consequences of Workplace Violence

In addition to the support and assistance available from various governmental and private agencies, public school employees have another powerful resource available to them. In the final analysis, this resource is often the most effective, manageable one of all. *It is their own personal, individual determination to protect themselves from injuries and illnesses arising from violence in the workplace.*

The first step is for the individual to decide there is a real need to gain both tangible protection and the peace of mind that comes from knowing such protection is in place. Once this decision is made, the task becomes selecting the best steps to take to achieve this protection. Assess, organize, take action!

Step One: Assess the Situation –

What is the actual potential for injury or illness arising from violence in your workplace? Consider the overall environment, including:

1. Age of students.

2. Class composition - single or dual gender students, and number of students in the class.

3. Past history of violence in your classes.

4. Past history of violence in the school.

5. Present official policy or philosophy of the school towards on-site violence.

6. Nature and extent of training provided to employees for dealing with workplace violence and its consequences.

7. Resources provided for preventing and responding to violent episodes.

8. Attitude of parents.

9. Subjective belief and attitudes - your "gut feeling" about how safe you are.

1. Age of Students

In nearly every period of human development and each culture, it has been recognized that individuals passing through puberty transmit their "growing pains" to the people around them. As children physically, mentally, and emotionally move to adulthood, they adjust with varying degrees of speed (and success) to their new status. In American society, this transition has generally equated with the later portions of junior high and high school.

Certainly, prevalent economic conditions, current involvement in a war, technological developments, and other societal factors tend to impact the nature and rate of the maturing process. However, it is apparent that the massive changes in technology and its products such as electronic communications have created not only a highly complex society, but also served to complicate the definition and perception of "children," "young adults," and "adolescence." In large degree, teachers can now expect children in the age range normally associated with pre-school classes (ages 3-5) to represent nominal threats of violence. However, consideration should be given to the potential for those in this age group to have infectious diseases inherited from, or transmitted by family and friends. Reasonable care such as frequent washing of the hands and removal and washing of clothing contaminated with bodily fluids before re-use should be taken. Bites and scratches should not be ignored.

Elementary school students (ages 6-8) should be considered as a more serious potential source of violence and BBP infections. Special attention should be paid to behavioral analysis recommendations presented earlier in this book. An unfortunate trend in our society is for violent or uncontrolled acts to come from children who have traditionally been less prone to this type of behavior. Also, children tend to be heavier, stronger, and larger than previous generations, which complicates dealing with them when physical contact occurs.

As has been repeatedly demonstrated, the likelihood of individuals in this age group to bring weapons or objects that can be used as weapons to school has also increased. To some degree, installation of metal detectors and security guards has helped to moderate this situation. However, many schools lack these concrete protective measures, especially elementary level schools. Finally, the widespread abuse and availability of controlled substances has now become a serious problem for elementary schools.

Junior high school students should be considered to represent the same degree of potentially violent behavior as high school students. In most schools the issues involved with prevalence of drugs and their consequent abuse, the frequency and severity of physical altercations, and other factors causing exposure of public school employees to injury or illness are similar between junior and senior high schools.

Statistically, the incidence of workplace violence is relatively small in colleges and universities. Most students are there voluntarily, and an increasing number of older students add stability. However, there have been some horrific recent college shootings: Dawson College in Montreal, Canada, and the University of Pittsburgh. Dawson College police and school officials stated that total results of the episode were believed to be far less severe than might have been the case thanks to improved training and communication between responders. The attention and resources being diverted to "Terror Prevention and Control" has increased dramatically. It is a valuable resource for school employees seeking to deal with violence on their campus.

2. Class Composition: Single Gender or Dual Gender Students and Number of Students in the Class

Overall, classes with both female and male student composition tend to have lower incidence of violent occurrences than in those with one sex or the other. In many situations, single sex classes are found in private schools or those affiliated with religious institutions.

In the same vein, violent behavior tends to be more frequent in classes with larger numbers of students. It may be that larger classes tend to make the individual student more "anonymous" and less inclined to feel like an active member of a group. Also, it may be that larger classes tend to move to a common denominator of performance that is below the satisfaction level of brighter and more aggressive students. Whatever the causal factors, larger classes represent a factor in assessing the potential for violent behavior.

3. Past History of Violence in your Classes

As in any profession, experience in the academic workplace reveals certain patterns of behavior among co-workers, people served, etc. Consequently, teachers and other school employees come to know that each season of the school year has certain common characteristics year-to-year. That certain times of the school day represent greater disciplinary problems, and that other patterns of behavior tend to emerge and are repeated. It is important for these patterns to be identified and analyzed to establish "critical points". For example, if experience shows that previous episodes have occurred primarily at a certain time of day, or day of the week, or just before or after a particular school event, it would be prudent to implement appropriate precautions such as available back-up personnel, specific pre-planning for separation of likely participants, etc.

Discussions with other school personnel may be helpful in gaining an accurate perspective on potential risks and effective methods of control.

4. Past History of Violence in the School

A related area of consideration is that of episodes of violence that have occurred in the school where you work. Although past experience is not an absolute predictor of future episodes, it can serve as an indicator of what form of violent behavior may occur and with what frequency. It also helps to focus attention on possible sources or causes of violent behavior, and may identify both individual students and groups of students who manifest erratic or violent behavior in the school. It allows thought, effort, and resources to be focused on trouble spots to help anticipate and prevent physical confrontations.

5. The Official Philosophy and Policies of the School Regarding On-Site Violence and Its Consequences

The ideal time to develop a core philosophy and policies is *before* an episode of on-site violence occurs. Any tendency to ignore or avoid the issue should be strongly resisted.

Certainly, it is inappropriate to exaggerate the problem, or develop excessively complex or punitive programs. On the other hand, preparation for workplace violence in a school is just as prudent and appropriate as traditional protection programs such as Fire Safety and Evacuation Procedures.

The basic program elements outlined below should be in place and all school personnel should be thoroughly familiar with them.

6. The Current Nature and Extent of Workplace Violence Response Training

The employee should objectively and honestly consider whether the type and amount of training provided for prevention and response to violent episodes is adequate. Questions should include:

1. Do I clearly understand what I should do to prevent a violent confrontation between students and students and myself from happening?

2. If the situation can't be prevented, how can I minimize it and limit results such as injuries?

3. Have enough people been trained to provide appropriate first aid care for cases where body fluids have been released? If outside sources are relied upon to respond to such cases, am I confident they will respond quickly enough?

4. Is there a response system in place to maximize my protection against Bloodborne Pathogen diseases, and do I fully understand how it works and what my entitlements are?

The answers to all of these questions should be an unequivocal **YES!**

7. The Resources Provided for Preventing and Responding to Violent Episodes

The defined philosophy and related policies previously discussed should specifically address the following requirements:

1. In-place agreements with public service organizations such as police, fire, ambulance, and community health care providers. Planning meetings should be held periodically to review response to on-site violence episodes as well as traditional issues such as fire, violent storms, flooding, etc.

2. An adequate number of first aid kits and supplemental supplies are maintained and periodically inspected to ensure protection of all people exposed to BBP sources.

3. Appropriate and adequate clean-up and containment materials and supplies are always available to ensure that garments, dressings, rags, and work surfaces can be effectively containerized or cleaned as appropriate.

8. Parental Attitudes

Although assessment of the potential attitudes and response of parents to a violent episode involving their child is necessarily subjective, some thought should be devoted to this issue. Teacher-parent conferences should include review of incidents that indicate the possibility of more serious incidents later. The purpose of considering this issue prior to an occurrence is to form at least a general idea as to what degree of parental support and involvement can be expected if an incident involving their child occurs.

It is prudent to document any meeting. It may be wise, depending upon the circumstances, to have another school representative such as the principal, vice-principal, dean, etc. present. At the very least these suggestions should be considered as part of evaluating the overall situation.

9. Subjective Belief and Attitudes - Your "Gut Feelings" about Your Personal Safety

After considering the factors listed previously, you should decide how you *really* feel about your situation. What is your overall assessment of the likelihood of being the victim of workplace violence that could result in physical injury or illness from exposure to Bloodborne Pathogens?

It may help if you consider the hazard in relation to other hazards that you and everyone else face such as tornadoes, auto accidents, crime, etc. Certainly, your exposure is less than that of police or fire personnel. However, you work in a unique environment with its own particular hazards. If your individual situation causes you to have serious concern about your safety, use review of these factors to pinpoint what specific improvements are needed. If you decide the potential for workplace violence is on a par with other acceptable risks that you face, then use the factor review to focus appropriate energy on strengthening weak spots to improve your chances of avoiding injury or illness.

Step Two: Methods for Gaining Improved Protection Against Workplace Violence and Injuries or Illness —

The Lonely Path - Do You Want to Lead or Follow?

Part of your assessment should include development of an objective assessment of your personal situation in relation to that of your co-workers. If you conclude that you face a significant threat, then you should decide how many others are similarly at hazard. Begin with a personal conversation with someone whom you trust. If your fears appear to be exaggerated, the sharing of perceptions may help you to resolve them.

If your co-worker shares your concerns, this initial conversation can lead to discussions with others who have similar concerns. In this event, a group will tend to form and leaders will emerge. Your personal degree of involvement should appear as part of this evolution. Bear in mind that definition of enlightened self-interest grows from exchange of ideas and perceptions. Try to keep an open mind to ideas that are new or seem extreme or unrealistic. Feel free to express your own perceptions. The consensus that emerges will represent the collective strength and abilities of people working together to solve common problems. It is a great truth that *None of Us is Smarter Than All of Us.*

One component of finding common cause is the amount of information and insight generated. Even a small group will find that its members have connections with other people who can be of great value to the project. For example, group members may have personal access to governmental authorities at various levels, key media representatives, or educational system administrators with knowledge and experience who will support sincere, legitimate requests for help in improving the safety and well-being of school employees.

If nothing else, a group is likely to receive more attention and support than a lone individual. The consensus that emerges lends strength and comfort to all the members of the group. Flexibility and effectiveness in dealing with frustrations and setbacks that occur in developing a satisfactory protection program also result.

The Role of Employee Unions

If you and your co-workers are represented by a union or other collective bargaining organization, you probably have a ready source of information and support. You may well find that a formal program for protection from workplace violence and related hazards already exists. Ideally, the program will be coordinated with an in-place school program.

If there are shortcomings and omissions in the program, you should be able to address these flaws through the union. At the very least, identification of what corrections and improvements are necessary should be easier.

Other benefits of a formal union-type organization in place include:

1. Access to legal counsel through the union.

2. Support in pressing claims for injuries or illnesses sustained.

3. Help in establishing effective protection and prevention measures.

In the event that you and your co-workers are not represented by a collective bargaining organization, you may wish to consider the merits of joining one. This topic is far outside the scope of this writing. However, review and discussion of the subject may help to clarify what you and your associates wish to do to best ensure your protection from workplace violence.

If you are represented by a collective bargaining organization, your discussions will help you to decide what requests and efforts must be made to gain support in your efforts, correct any deficiencies, and strengthen any weaknesses.

Conclusion

It is quite likely you currently have some information and insight into the issues discussed in this chapter. Hopefully, you can now obtain a clearer picture of the issues involved and decide what additional information is needed to define your current personal potential exposure to acts of violence and risks of injury or illness. Once you have assessed the situation, you can develop an action plan and begin working to implement it.

EPILOGUE:
Bloodborne Pathogen Protection – At A Glance

1. Always Protect Yourself – Don't touch an injured person until you put on gloves. Use an airway or other protective device when giving mouth-to-mouth resuscitation.

2. Wash Your Hands, clothing, etc. with soap and water THOROUGHLY if another person's Body Fluids contact them.

3. Seek qualified medical advice if you are exposed to the body fluids of another person.

Those At Greatest Risk:

1. Teachers, teacher's aides, bus drivers, driver's aides, maintenance personnel.

2. Custodians, voluntary infrequent first aid administrators.

3. Administrative Staff: technicians, engineers, EDI / MIS personnel.

Maximum Protection – Universal Precautions:

1. Engineering Controls / Work Practices – Insist on having facilities for washing hands and designated waste disposal facilities for body fluid-soiled clothing and other materials.

2. Personal Protective Equipment (PPE) – Latex or vinyl gloves, mouth shields for mouth-to-mouth resuscitation,

disposable face masks, aprons, or coats.

3. Housekeeping — insist on regular sanitization of designated "Care Stations" — receptacles for contaminated clothing / materials; separate storage facilities for food and drink outside of "Care Stations;" and NO eating or drinking in "Care Stations."

4. Obtain a combination of initial medical evaluation and follow-up examinations as necessary by a competent physician — including Hepatitis "B" innoculations if necessary.

Information / Training:

1. *What* — Review of causes and symptoms of BBP — Transmission routes — Protection plan elements – Identify possible exposure situations — Appropriate PPE: Where stored, when and how to use it; and where and how to dispose of it safely.

2. *When* — Initial assignment of a new work environment, annually.

Chapter Nine

The Application of the OSHA BBP Standard and the Public Scholastic Workplace

You have a general impression that OSHA is a federal agency and that the OSHAct provides certain protections to workers in industry. However, you are unsure whether or not the agency or the act applies to teachers and other school employees. You're not even sure the issue of potential illnesses arising from Bloodborne Pathogens (BBP) is addressed by the agency or the Act. In order to decide on an action plan, you need some specific, useful information. Where do you go? What do you do?

Key Concepts and Data in this Chapter

- The Federal Department of Labor-Occupational Safety & Health Safety Standard (DOL/OSHA).

- The Background of The Federal Standard.

- The Elements of The Federal Standard.

- Application of The Standard in the Academic Workplace.

The Background of the Federal Standard

The DOL/OSHA Standard appears in Subpart Z — Toxic and Hazardous Substances, 29 CFR 1910.1030, effective March 6, 1992 (III-I). *Note:* Employers subject to the Standard were required to have the Exposure Control Plan required by the Standard in place on or before March 5, 1992 (111-2). *How does this affect you?*

The Standard was publicized in response to a growing awareness (and concern) of increasing infection rates in the medical care industry from exposure to Bloodborne Pathogens (BBP). The incidence of various strains of Hepatitis as well as actual and anticipated Human Immunodeficiency Virus **(HIV)** cases amongst health care workers caused the DOL/OSHA Administration to respond by including this Standard in the body of OSHA Regulations.

Although the initial motivation for creating the Standard was the exposure of health care workers, it was organized labor, workers in related industries, and public concern that caused the definition of *Employer* and *Affected Employee* to be expanded. Now, enterprises subject to the provisions of the Standard Act included those whose employees had a visible exposure to infected bodily fluids.

Since the initial effective date of the Bloodborne Pathogens Standard, there have been numerous interpretations and guidelines provided by DOL/OSHA. Specifically, additional protection from *"sharps"* (Infected needles, broken glass products, test tubes, etc.) is required. More extensive and detailed record keeping of actual and potential exposure incidents must be implemented. Otherwise, requirements of the Standard remain unchanged. As was discussed in Chapter Three, the various state plans are required to implement standard elements *equal to or more extensive than* the federal standard. Therefore, the requirements of state Bloodborne Pathogen Standards have followed federal requirements.

The Elements of the Federal Standard

The Bloodborne Pathogens Standard consists of nine elements. They are listed (as a-I) in keeping with the format used in all DOL/OSHA Standards. (The Standard text is on the OSHA website: www.osha.gov, available at any OSHA regional or field office, or at your public library.) The DOL/OSHA General Industry Standards may be purchased from the Government Printing Office (GPO). The BBP Standard of a given state or territory with its own approved federal OSHA equivalent plan can be obtained from that state authority. The Elements of a state's plan may vary somewhat from the federal standard, but the essential requirements are the same. Certain states (California) have more extensive requirements and a broader definition of employer/employee obligations.

Because of the easy access to the Standards, this chapter focuses on the applications of the BBP Standard as it relates to you, the *Scholastic Workplace Employee*. For continuity and ease of understanding, we'll follow the Standard Outline and be referenced to the subpart being discussed.

The federal OSHA Standard addressing BBP illnesses and the mandated prevention and protection requirements is structured to ease the understanding of the issues and location of information sources. Scholastic workplace employees are strongly encouraged to familiarize themselves with the provisions of this Standard and how they relate to their specific site.

1. Scope and Application - Section (a).

This Section establishes the applicability of the Standard to all occupational exposures to blood and other potentially infectious materials, as spelled-out in the Definitions Section which follows. This Section does not address "Employer," either as a defined term or as a source of program protections. *However, all state plans do include public schools as "Employers."* Public school employees should bear this in mind when seeking regulatory protection. As discussed in Chapter Eight, *all states are required to provide equal protection to public school employees, even though public schools are not subject to direct federal enforcement activity, and may not be subject to proposed penalties in some jurisdictions.*

2. Definitions - Section (b).

Certain specific definitions were extracted from this Section to illustrate basic concepts of exposure and illness related to BBPs. There are two definitions (A and B) with special significance to school employees.

A. Exposure Incident – *Means a specific eye, mouth, other mucous membrane, non-intact skin, or parental contact with blood or other potentially infectious materials resulting from the performance of the employee's duties.* Should a school employee be physically assaulted by a student, or while attempting to deal with a physical contact episode between students, there IS a possibility of an exposure incident occurring (II-I).

B. Regulated Waste – *Means liquid (or semi-liquid) blood or other potentially infectious materials, contaminated items that would release blood or other potentially infectious materials in a liquid or semi-liquid state if compressed; items caked with dried blood or other potentially infectious materials and capable of releasing these materials during handling, contaminated sharps and pathological and microbial wastes containing blood or other infectious materials.*

One of the most common areas of deficiency in BBP control programs is the failure to provide provisions for the clean-up, containment and proper disposal of contaminated materials. Both immediate containment and storage of such waste and its ultimate disposal in an approved disposal site must be provided for in the program.

3. Exposure Control - Section (c).

A primary requirement of the Standard is that a **written** Exposure Control Plan be developed by the employer, kept current and communicated to it's employees. The plan must "eliminate or minimize employee exposure" (II-2). The plan must contain, at a minimum, specific lists of job classifications which have frequent or regular exposure to BBP hazards, occasional exposure to BBP hazards; or minimal occupational exposure to BBP hazards, as well as specific tasks or procedures which involve such exposures.

Although this requirement was developed with health care and medical service personnel in mind, the potential exposure of scholastic workplace employees to such hazards makes it appropriate for the program to be in place in schools. A specimen written program appears as Appendix B.

Common "real world" deficiencies in this portion of the program include (1) failure to perform an annual review and resultant revision of the plan, and (2) the failure to maintain required individual employee medical records as set forth in 29CFR 1910.1020, access to employee exposure and medical records. Section (c) specifically requires that this requirement be met.

4. Methods of Compliance - Section (d).

It should be noted that this Section is the source of the requirements for both employers and employees to set in place and follow the philosophy of "Universal Precautions." This concept requires that appropriate physical facilities be provided by the employer to allow immediate access to thorough washing of any or all parts of the body exposed to bodily fluids of others. Hot water and soap-bearing facilities are the preferred option to meet this requirement.

In addition, this Section presents the mandated interaction between engineering, administrative and Personal Protective Equipment (PPE) methods to ensure optimum protection of employees. Particular attention should be given to Section (d) (2): Engineering and Work Practice Controls that sets forth specific requirements for hand washing facilities and specifies that "where occupational exposure remains after institution of these controls, Personal Protective Equipment shall also be used" (11-3).

Section (d) (3) contains all the particulars concerning PPE, and should be reviewed in light of the specific workplace characteristics involved. From this review; omissions, deficiencies and suitability of equipment provided can be established.

Section (d) (4) (iv) dealing with Housekeeping Requirements (including provisions for proper handling of contaminated waste) should be compared to exposures, current arrangements and perceived needs. To ensure comprehensive compliance with this Section, it should be verified that the employer has arranged for off-site, waste handling support services to be aware that they may be asked to dispose of potentially BBP-contaminated waste. They must be able to verify that they, in turn will dispose of such materials properly.

5. HIV and HBV Research Laboratories and Production Facilities Section (e).

The provisions of this Section do not apply directly to the scholastic workplace unless a research laboratory dedicated to work with HIV or HBV agents is located on-site. Such a facility is required to comply fully with all provisions of the applicable federal and/or state safety and health standard as well as related standards. Since this book is intended for the protection of individuals not involved in such specific activities, it will only be said that all related site-specific regulations and requirements should be scrupulously followed. Also, the expertise and assistance of managers and employees of the facility should be sought in developing protection for the rest of the scholastic facility.

6. Hepatitis B Vaccination and Post-Exposure Evaluation and Follow-up - Section (f).

The essential consideration in this Section is its stipulation that employees are entitled to Hepatitis B Vaccination(s) (HBV) at no cost to them if such a procedure is warranted because of workplace exposure to this disease. Specifically, guidelines are provided for the following procedures:

  A. Testing of the individual after an Exposure Incident.

  B. Hepatitis Vaccination if deemed necessary as a result of such testing.

  C. Post-Exposure Evaluation and Follow-up.

Notice that in this Section, sub-Section (3) (i-vi), the employer is required to provide Post-Exposure Evaluation and Follow-Up. In addition to the requirement that all such information be kept confidential, such evaluation must include:

  A. Documentation of the route(s) of exposure and circumstances under which the exposure occurred.

  B. Identification and documentation of the source individual, unless the employer can establish that identification is infeasible or prohibited by state or local law.

C. Collection and testing of blood for HBV and HIV serological status.

D. Post-exposure prophylaxis, when medically indicated, as recommended by the U.S. Public Health Service.

This Section of the Standard includes a lengthy discussion of (1) the rights of the victim of the assault leading to exposure to BBP disease in relation to (2) the legal rights of the infected perpetrator of the assault to anonymity under state and local laws in the jurisdiction involved. In the event of an occurrence, the assault victim should consult with an attorney for specific legal advice as to their rights in the matter.

In addition to the rights and entitlements of the victim, this Section of the Standard also includes the related obligation of the employer to provide certain information to the health care professional who provides treatment and care to the assault victim. Section (4)(i-ii), Information Provided to the Healthcare Professional includes this information.

In Section (5), Healthcare Professional's Written Opinion, it is important to note that the *Employer* is required to "obtain and provide the *Employee* with a copy of the evaluating healthcare professional's written opinion within 15 days of the completion of the evaluation"(II-4). This point is raised to underscore the fact that the employer is required to take an active role in maximizing the health and safety of the employee, and function as a partner in meeting this objective.

The employee has the right to decline receiving vaccinations for Hepatitis B at the time of the event that may have led to infection. The employee is required to complete a written document rejecting such vaccinations. (A copy of a form meeting the requirements of the Standard appears as Appendix "A" in the Standard.) If later the employee decides to receive vaccinations, the employer is required to provide such medical service at no charge to the employee, and all rights of confidentiality, retention of records, etc. as they appear in this portion of the Standard still apply.

The final area of employee rights and protection is set forth in Section (6): Medical Record Keeping, which stipulates that all medical records required by the Standard be maintained as set forth in Section (h) of the Standard (Section 8 of this review).

7. Communication of Hazards to Employees - Section (g).

It may be helpful to scholastic workplace employees to remember that the type of information required to be provided under this Section of the standard is valuable to both themselves and the students, parents and other members of their community. The more knowledgeable all parties are, the better this important public health issue can be managed.

However, the presence of labels and signs can be extremely alarming to individuals who are unaware of their intent and purpose. Misuse or absence of appropriate labels and signs can lead to improper recognition of hazards or improper control of contaminated materials. The entire label and signage program should be explained and understood by everyone.

Finally, the Information and Training requirements of this Standard can be used to maximize the individual's awareness and effectiveness in dealing with the issues involved. On a more personal note, the better all stakeholders understand the nature of BBP illness that can arise from physical assault, the more effectively they can work together to deal with this complex and difficult problem. Ideally, scholastic workplace employees become members of a closely-knit team, rather than potential victims.

Within Section (g)(7), the topics of Labels, Signs, Information and Training are addressed. Remember: these topics are structured to provide specific guidance regarding the hazards of BBP exposure. As discussed previously, the requirements are intended to be integrated with other labeling and training requirements of safety and health standards to enhance and ensure employee health and safety.

Labels and Containers

Labels of a very specific format and color are required to be affixed to "containers of regulated waste, refrigerators and freezers containing blood or other potentially infectious material; and other containers used to store, transport, or ship blood and other potentially infectious materials ... " Section (g)(1)(i). This portion of the Section also sets forth requirements/specifications for containers and bags. Both labels and containers are required to be fluorescent orange or orange-red colored and bear the legend:

BIOHAZARD

The requirements further include provisions for ensuring that Biohazard labels be attached to containers with "string, wire, adhesive, or other method that prevents their loss or unintentional removal" (II-5).

Although this portion of the Standard is predominantly addressed to worksites where equipment, materials and blood/body fluids are regularly handled, *it has specific significance to scholastic workplace employees.* Precisely because exposure to potentially BBP-contaminated substances is not a well-recognized hazard in schools. Appropriate supplies and training in the management of such substances may not be in place when needed. It is *very important* that leak-resistant biohazard bags or other sealable containers be readily available to any exposed person so the concept of Universal Precautions can be successfully applied.

Additionally, biohazard labels should be available to properly and accurately identify any item that cannot be placed in a biohazard container. This precaution will greatly reduce exposure of personnel assigned to clean up exposure areas, and also ensure optimum decontamination of equipment, work areas, etc.

Signs

The Standard requires that all facilities engaged in work that involves potential or actual exposure to HBV or HIV-bearing substances be clearly identified with signs at the site entrance displaying:

   A. The biohazard logo and the words BIOHAZARD and the name of the infectious agent on a fluorescent orange or red-orange background.

   B. Special requirements for entering the area.

   C. Name and telephone number(s) of appropriate contact person(s).

It would be wise to designate a suitable storage room, closet, locker or cabinet to serve as a storage facility for contaminated materials until they can be properly disposed of. Only an area that can be readily and effectively decontaminated should be selected.

*Under **NO** circumstances should a refrigerator or freezer be used to store contaminated materials or be used to store **any other** materials (food, etc.).*

Training

To ensure that employees who may be exposed to HBV or HIV agents are protected, the Standard requires that adequate training be provided at no cost to the employee during working hours. Although the extent of training is in proportion to the nature and extent of exposure, there are certain primary *areas that must be addressed* in the training program. They are:

Frequency of Training Required

    A. At the time of initial assignment to tasks where occupational exposure may take place.

    B. Within 90 days after the effective date of the Standard.

    C. At least annually thereafter – annual training for all employees shall be provided within one year of their previous training (11-6). The employer is required to provide training tailored to the specific nature of exposure the employee faces. Supplemental or periodic training must address modifications of tasks or procedures, new tasks and any procedure that affects the employee's occupational exposure. It is reasonable to assume that any new knowledge or information concerning BBP diseases must also be included in the training of employees who may need this information for their protection.

    D. Training materials are to be appropriate in content and vocabulary to the educational level, literacy and language of employees.

Training Program Elements

The Standard stipulates that the obligatory training program contain 14 elements. You are urged to review the actual language outlining the course content requirements of each element to determine what additions, modifications or supplemental materials are necessary to optimize the value of their specific training profile. Note there are additional requirements for training at sites with laboratories or other facilities that handle HIV or HBV-bearing substances. A review of training program elements as they impact academic workplace employees follows:

1. Text of the Standard

The core element of the program is a copy of the regulatory text of the Standard. The employer is required to have this document accessible to all employees. It is prudent to conduct an annual audit of the entire program. This audit should include verification that a copy of the most current text is on hand. Training materials should be reviewed at the same time and updated as necessary. The best way to ensure the program and its materials are current is to assign specific responsibility for monitoring developments in BBP disease control to a specific person by title and by name. Of course, any significant developments should be conveyed to all parties as soon as possible.

2. Epidemiology and Symptoms of BBP Diseases

Diseases caused by BBP agents are discussed in the text of the Standard. However, there is much information available from the Center for Disease Control, federal and state health departments, local care providers, local libraries, etc. It is a good idea to have a representative of a local care provider such as hospital, clinic, specialist physician, etc. address all site personnel to review the issues involved and answer questions. A written summary of the proceedings should be kept in the Training File for reference and to help satisfy this requirement.

3. Explanation of BBP Modes of Transmission

As noted previously, this topic is addressed in the text of the Standard. Additional information is also available from the sources listed. Whatever the source, training must include a review of this Modes of Transmission subject.

4. Elements of the Employer's Exposure Control Plan

This Plan with its various elements should be maintained in a specified on-site location, along with all necessary support documentation. *It is not necessary* for all documentation such as medical records, training records, transportation and disposal documentation, etc. to be in one physical location. However, the Plan should include information on where all data is located onsite.

In addition, it is prudent to have specific responsibility assigned to an individual (by title and name) for maintenance of the program and knowledge of where all related documentation is located. Copies of the basic plan should be available to any employee wanting one. The Plan and the name of the person(s) to contact for a copy must be included in the training program.

5. Review of Tasks, Activities or Circumstances in Which an Employee May be Exposed to BBP

Various personnel may be exposed to substances or materials containing BBP. Teachers and other personnel may suffer physical assaults or contact with body fluids of contaminated persons. Custodians and maintenance staff may have to deal with collection and cleaning-up contaminated materials or equipment. Bus drivers, teacher's aides, cafeteria and administrative personnel can all be exposed. Examples of all such potential exposures must be established, documented and included in the training program.

6. Review of Protective Methods to Limit/Prevent Exposure to BBP

The concept of Universal Precautions must be reviewed. Information on the relative effectiveness of Engineering Controls, Administrative Methods and Personal Protective Equipment (PPE) must also be reviewed, along with a discussion of how the three elements are expected to interact.

7. In-Depth Discussion of the Types, Proper Use, Location, Removal, Handling, Decontamination and Disposal of PPE

Because of the heavy emphasis on PPE as the "first line of defense against BBP exposure," it is ***very important*** that all potentially exposed employees be fully knowledgeable about all aspects of this subject. The theoretical concepts involved plus practical information on storage and disposal issues, and actual hands-on training in the actual "donning, doffing, use, and disposal" of this equipment must be performed. All training must be documented, and the documentation retained as part of the training program files.

8. An Explanation of the Basis for Selection of PPE

Selection of Personal Protective Equipment is based upon compliance with the specific requirements of the Standard (which effectively prescribes the type of PPE planned for use). Site-specific considerations also enter in - the actual nature and extent of exposure to potentially infected substances. PPE selection is impacted by:

- Who is expected to be exposed based upon employment duty profiles and resultant high hazard tasks.

- Past experiences with physical assaults.

- School policies governing physical contact with potentially infected persons.

- Types of engineering controls in place for collection.

- Containment and disposal of potentially and actually contaminated materials.

- Overall objective decisions on how to limit overall exposure.

The **Ultimate Goal** is to consider all these factors and select types of PPE that strike a balance between appropriate protection and effective storage, availability and ease of use. The cost of all PPE should be considered in light of suitability, durability, shelf life and overall protection provided. The cheapest equipment is *rarely* capable of meeting these criteria.

9. Information about the Hepatitis B Vaccine, including Information on its Efficacy, Safety, Method of Administration, The Benefits of Being Vaccinated, and the Vaccination will be Free

Employees are entitled to vaccine inoculations for treatment of Hepatitis "B" contracted from occurrences in the workplace.

Employees are required to provide such treatment at no charge to the employee. Therefore, it is important that factual information concerning the process be provided to *all* employees. This information may be obtained from the Standard as well as the sources listed earlier in this book.

Important: The Standard does not address other forms of Hepatitis that may be contracted in the workplace under certain conditions. The individual should discuss these other forms of Hepatitis with a qualified healthcare provider. It may be appropriate to negotiate care for these forms of the disease with the employer as part of the specific program for the site.

10. Appropriate Actions to Take and People to Contact in an Emergency involving Blood or other Potentially Infectious Materials

Information for this training should be drawn from the written site plan. It is important that contact persons be identified by title and name, with their telephone, pager or other communication information being provided. Contact lists and related information must be kept current, with all employees having ready access to this data. Training must include clear, practical methods for dealing with physical injuries, as well as containment and proper disposal of contaminated waste.

11. The Procedure to follow if an Exposure Incident occurs, Including the Method of Reporting the Incident and the Medical Follow-up that will be made Available

Training for this topic should include:

   A. Procedure for immediate reporting, i.e. direct, by telephone, etc.

   B. Person(s) to whom the immediate report should be made.

   C. Medical source to contact for care.

D. Written report procedures and forms to be used.

12. The Post-Exposure Evaluation and Follow-up the Employer is Required to Provide to the Employee following an Exposure Incident

Employees are entitled to receive complete information about their entitlements resulting from an exposure incident in which they have suffered actual or potential infection of a BBP-induced disease. Specifically, this training should include:

A. Full explanation of the Hepatitis "B" inoculation cycle.

B. Employee's right to refuse the Hepatitis B inoculation(s).

C. Documentation and appropriate forms for recording the incident medical data.

D. Employee rights related to the medical status of those who physically attacked them.

13. Signs, Labels and/or Color Coding Required by the Standard

All site personnel need to be familiar with the significance of the Biohazard Marking, the distinctive, fluorescent orange or red-orange waste containers and labels bearing these Biohazard Marking colors. They must be advised to use these materials only for the storage of infectious waste, and such waste must not be placed in any other type of container. Clear instruction must also be provided concerning the use of refrigerators and other storage facilities, emphasizing that contaminated waste storage facilities must *NOT* be used for any other purpose.

14. An Opportunity for Interactive Questions and Answers with the Training Session Instructor

For the trainer to maximize effectiveness, it is very important that all participants have the opportunity to ask questions, clarify technical points, and share information. Handouts, to include Frequently Asked Questions (FAQs), etc. are always helpful. This approach ensures that all participants consider themselves program stakeholders. It also ensures that impractical practices and awkward procedures are corrected based upon the "real world" knowledge of the participants, thereby optimizing the effectiveness of the program.

This Interactive Q&A portion of the Standard also stipulates in Section (g) (2) (viii) that "The person conducting the training shall be knowledgeable in the subject matter covered by the Elements contained in the training program as it relates to the workplace that the training will address." This requirement imposes an employer obligation that the trainer be fully familiar with the Standard and its requirements, as well as the specific requirements and needs of the specific worksheet.

Specific information about BBP Protection Training Programs is available from federal and state agencies, plus numerous private safety, health and environmental compliance training firms. A list of such sources appears as Appendix A in this book. A policy statement appears as Appendix B in this book.

15. Record Keeping

This portion of the standard has four (4) Records Sections: Medical, Training, Requirements Governing Availability of Records, and Transfer of Records (from a current employer to a new employer). Because the Standard is so essentially concerned about employee medical status with regard to BBP Agents exposure, it is closely tied to, and interrelated with 29 CFR 1910.1020: Access to Employee Exposure and Medical Records. Because there is a possibility of scholastic workplace employees transferring from one academic site to another, it is important that provisions for medical records transfer be ensured. This federal standard makes the transfer of medical records *obligatory*.

It would be wise for the employee of any school to verify that a system for maintaining medical records from site to site is in place. They should also verify that transfer of records is included in the system, and that appropriate confidentiality and other privacy protection is in place. Naturally, such provisions should not interfere with accessibility of medical information to professional care providers and other persons on a need-to-know basis.

Medical Records

The Standard requires that the Employer maintain medical records containing:

    A. Employee name and social security number.

    B. A copy of Employee's Hepatitis "B" vaccination records (if applicable).

    C. Copies of all examination, medical testing and follow-up procedures as relates to B (above).

    D. Employer's copy of health care provider's report(s) on B (above).

    E. Employer's copies of all required reports to health care providers on B (above).

F. Confidentiality: All records are to be kept Confidential. They may be released only as provided by law, with the expressed, written consent of the employee where discretionary.

All medical records are to be maintained by the employer for a period of at least the duration of employment +*30* years.

Training Records

The Standard requires that the employer shall maintain training records that contain:

A. Training session dates.

B. Contents or a summary of contents of training sessions.

C. Names and qualifications of course instructors.

D. Names and job titles of all persons who attended the sessions.

Training records are to be maintained for three (3) years from the date the training occurred.

Availability of Records

Both medical and training records are to be made available to the Assistant Secretary of Labor and/or to the Director of the Region (who has jurisdiction over the site) for review and copying. In state-approved plans, the comparable authority has this right also. The employee (or their designated representative who has their written consent) may have access to the employee's records, in addition to the authorities previously listed.

Transfer of Records

The Employer may transfer records under the same provisions set forth in sub-part (h) of 29 CFR 1910.1020. This regulation stipulates maintenance of such records for the duration of employment + 30 years, and requires successor employers to maintain the chain of custody unbroken. In cases where operations are not transferred, provision is made for the transfer of such records to the National Institute for Occupational Safety & Health (NIOSH).

Important: It would again be prudent for the scholastic workplace employee to verify that their employer is in compliance with these provisions of the Standard.

Application of the Standard Within the Academic Workplace

Although the Standard was primarily developed to protect employees in workplaces engaged in medical care services, it has been well established that the diseases caused by Bloodborne Pathogens represent a real threat **to all** American workers. The serious symptoms of these diseases, as well as the fact that is no known cure for some of them, make these precautions necessary.

Fortunately, the provisions of the Standard are flexible enough to allow them to be adapted to the academic workplace. You should read through the regulations and requirements for a protection program, evaluate the current protections in place, and, develop an action plan to correct weaknesses and deficiencies.

Although much effort by everyone at all workplace staff levels may be required, the result will be an environment less susceptible to violence and potential exposure to life-threatening diseases.

Appendix A – Directory of States with Approved Occupational Safety and Health Plans

(http://www.osha.gov/oshdir/states.html)

Alaska Department of Labor and Workforce Development
P.O. Box 111149
Juneau, Alaska 99811-1149
1111 W. 8th Street, Room 308
Juneau, Alaska 99801-1149
Greg O'Claray, Commissioner (907) 465-2700 Fax: (907) 465-2784
Grey Mitchell, Director (907) 465-4855 Fax: (907) 465-6012

Industrial Commission of Arizona
800 W. Washington
Phoenix, Arizona 85007-2922
Larry Etchechury, Director, ICA(602) 542-4411 Fax: (602) 542-1614
Darin Perkins, Program Director (602) 542-5795 Fax: (602) 542-1614

California Department of Industrial Relations
1515 Clay Street, Suite 1901
Oakland, California 94612
John Rea, Acting Director (415) 703-5050 Fax:(415) 703-5059
Len Welsh, Acting Chief, Cal/OSHA (510) 286-7000 FAX (510) 286-7038
Vicky Heza, Deputy Chief, Cal/OSHA (714) 939-8093 FAX (714) 939-8094

Connecticut Department of Labor
200 Folly Brook Boulevard
Wethersfield, Connecticut 06109
Patricia H. Mayfield, Commissioner (860) 566-5123 Fax: (860) 566-1520

Conn-OSHA
38 Wolcott Hill Road
Wethersfield, Connecticut 06109
Richard Palo, Director (860) 263-6900 Fax: (860) 263-6940

Hawaii Department of Labor and Industrial Relations
830 Punchbowl Street
Honolulu, Hawaii 96813
Nelson B. Befitel, Director (808) 586-8844 Fax: (808) 586-9099

Indiana Department of Labor
State Office Building
402 West Washington Street, Room W195
Indianapolis, Indiana 46204-2751
Miguel Rivera, Commissioner (317) 232-2378 Fax: (317) 233-3790
Tim Grogg, Deputy Commissioner (317) 233-3605 Fax: (317) 233-3790

Iowa Division of Labor
1000 E. Grand Avenue
Des Moines, Iowa 50319-0209
Dave Neil, Commissioner (515) 281-3447 Fax: (515) 281-4698
Mary L. Bryant, Administrator (515) 281-3469 Fax: (515) 281-7995

Kentucky Department of Labor
1047 U.S. Highway 127 South, Suite 4
Frankfort, Kentucky 40601
Philip P. Anderson, Commissioner(502) 564-3070 Fax: (502) 564-5387
Stephen L. Morrison, Executive Director, Office of Occupational Safety & Health
(502) 564-3070 Fax: (502) 564-1682

Maryland Division of Labor and Industry
Department of Labor, Licensing and Regulation
1100 North Eutaw Street, Room 613
Baltimore, Maryland 21201-2206
Robert Lawson, Commissioner (410) 767-2241 Fax: (410) 767-2986
Jack English, Assistant Commissioner, MOSH (410) 767-2190 Fax: (410) 333-7747

Michigan Department of Labor and Economic Growth
Robert Swanson, Director
Michigan Occupational Safety and Health Administration
P.O. Box 30643
Lansing, MI 48909-8143
Doug Kalinowski, Director (517) 322-1814 Fax: (517) 322-1775
Martha Yoder, Deputy Director for Enforcement
(517) 322-1817 Fax: (517) 322-1775

Minnesota Department of Labor and Industry
443 Lafayette Road
St. Paul, Minnesota 55155
Scott Brener, Commissioner (651) 284-5010 Fax: (651) 282-5405
Patricia Todd, Assistant Commissioner (651) 284-5371 Fax: (651) 282-2527
Jeff Isakson, Administrative Director, OSHA Management Team
(651) 284-5372 Fax: (651) 297-2527

Nevada Division of Industrial Relations
400 West King Street, Suite 400
Carson City, Nevada 89703
Roger Bremmer, Administrator (775) 684-7260 Fax: (775) 687-6305
Occupational Safety and Health Enforcement Section (OSHES)
1301 N. Green Valley Parkway
Henderson, Nevada 89014
Tom Czehowski, Chief Administrative Officer (702) 486-9168 Fax: (702) 486-9020
[Las Vegas (702) 687-5240]

New Jersey Department of Labor and Workforce Development
Office of Public Employees Occupational Safety & Health (PEOSH)
1 John Fitch Plaza
P.O. Box 386
Trenton, NJ 08625-0386
Thomas D. Carver, Acting Commissioner (609) 292-2975 Fax: (609) 633-9271
Leonard Katz, Assistant Commissioner (609) 292-2313 Fax: (609) 695-1314
Howard Black, Director, PSOSH (609) 292-0501 Fax: (609) 292-3749
Gary Ludwig, Director, Occupational Health Service (609) 984-1843
   Fax: (609) 984-0849

New Mexico Environment Department
1190 St. Francis Drive, Suite 4050
P.O. Box 26110
Santa Fe, New Mexico 87502
Ron Curry, Jr., Secretary (505) 827-2850 Fax: (505) 827-2836
Butch Tongate, Bureau Chief (505) 476-8700 Fax: (505) 476-8734

New York Department of Labor
New York Public Employee Safety and Health Program
State Office Campus Building 12, Room 158
Albany, New York 12240
Linda Angello, Commissioner (518) 457-2741 Fax: (518) 457-6908
Anthony Germano, Director, Division of Safety and Health
   (518) 457-3518; Fax: (518) 457-1519
Maureen Cox, Program Manager (518) 457-1263 Fax: (518) 457-5545

North Carolina Department of Labor
4 West Edenton Street
Raleigh, North Carolina 27601-1092
Cherie Berry, Commissioner (919) 733-0359 Fax: (919) 733-1092
Allen McNeely, Deputy Commissioner, OSH Director (919) 807-2861
   Fax: (919) 807-2855
Kevin Beauregard, OSH Assistant Director (919) 807-2863 Fax: (919) 807-2856

Oregon Occupational Safety and Health Division
Department of Consumer and Business Services
350 Winter Street, NE, Room 430
Salem, Oregon 97301-3882
Michael Wood, Administrator (503) 378-3272 Fax: (503) 947-7461
Michele Patterson, Deputy Administrator (503) 378-3272 Fax: (503) 947-7461
David Sparks, Special Assistant for Federal & External Affairs (503) 378-3272
   Fax: (503) 947-7461

Puerto Rico Department of Labor
Prudencio Rivera Martínez Building
505 Muñoz Rivera Avenue
Hato Rey, Puerto Rico 00918
Roman M. Velasco Gonzalez, Secretary
(787) 754-2119 Fax: (787) 753-9550
José Droz-Alvarado, Assistant Secretary for Occupational Safety and Health
(787) 756-1100 / (787) 754-2171 Fax: (787) 767-6051

South Carolina Department of Labor, Licensing, and Regulation
Koger Office Park, Kingstree Building
110 Centerview Drive
PO Box 11329
Columbia, South Carolina 29211
Adrienne R. Youmans, Director (803) 896-4300 Fax: (803) 896-4393
Dottie Ison, Administrator (803) 896-7665 Fax: (803) 896-7670
Office of Voluntary Programs (803) 896-7744 Fax: (803) 896-7750

Tennessee Department of Labor and Workforce Development
710 James Robertson Parkway
Nashville, Tennessee 37243-0659
James G. Neeley, Commissioner (615) 741-2582 Fax: (615) 741-5078
John Winkler, Program Director (615) 741-2793 Fax: (615) 741-3325

Utah Labor Commission
160 East 300 South, 3rd Floor
PO Box 146650
Salt Lake City, Utah 84114-6650
Sherrie M. Hayashi, Commissioner (801) 530-6848 Fax: (801) 530-7906
Larry Patrick, Administrator (801) 530-6898 Fax: (801) 530-6390

Vermont Department of Labor
National Life Building - Drawer 20
Montpelier, Vermont 05620-3401
Patricia Moulton Powden, Commissioner (802) 828-4301 Fax: (802) 888-4022

Vermont OSHA
National Life Building - Drawer 20
Montpelier, Vermont 05620-3401
Robert McLeod, VOSHA Compliance Program Manager (802) 828-2765
Fax: (802) 828-2195

Virgin Islands Department of Labor
3012 Golden Rock
Christiansted, St. Croix, Virgin Islands 00820-4660
Cecil R. Benjamin, Commissioner (340) 773-1994 Fax: (340) 773-1858
John Sheen, Assistant Commissioner (340) 772-1315 Fax: (340) 772-4323
Francine Lang, Program Director (340) 772-1315 Fax: (340) 772-4323

Virginia Department of Labor and Industry
Powers-Taylor Building
13 South 13th Street
Richmond, Virginia 23219
C. Raymond Davenport, Commissioner (804) 786-2377 Fax: (804) 371-6524
Glenn Cox, Director, Safety Compliance, VOSHA (804) 786-2391 Fax: (804) 371-6524
Jay Withrow, Director, Office of Legal Support (804) 786-9873 Fax: (804) 786-8418

Washington Department of Labor and Industries
General Administration Building
PO Box 44001
Olympia, Washington 98504-4001

7273 Linderson Way SW
Tumwater, WA 98501-5414
Gary K. Weeks, Director (360) 902-4200 Fax: (360) 902-4202
Steve Cant, Assistant Director [PO Box 44600]
(360) 902-5495 Fax: (360) 902-5529
Program Manager, Federal-State Operations [PO Box 44600]
(360) 902-5430 Fax: (360) 902-5529

Wyoming Department of Employment
Workers' Safety and Compensation Division
Cheyenne Business Center
1510 East Pershing Boulevard
Cheyenne, Wyoming 82002
Gary W. Child, Administrator (307) 777-7700 Fax: (307) 777-5524
J.D. Danni, OSHA Program Manager (307) 777-7786 Fax: (307) 777-3646

Appendix B – SAMPLE Workplace Violence Policy Statement
(Sample Format)

(School Name) does not permit acts of violence or threats of violence on its premises. This prohibition includes ANY violent action including, but not limited to threatening verbal or written language, threatening gestures, or physical assault by any person on another. ALL types of weapons are prohibited anywhere on the property, and in school vehicles of all types. The only exception to this prohibition is weapons carried by law enforcement officials and officers of governmental agencies duly licensed to carry such weapons in the course of official duty. All school personnel, students, and visitors are required to adhere to this policy. Any infraction is to be reported to (designated person{s})immediately

(School Name) is firmly committed to the protection of staff members, students and legitimate visitors from acts of violence. We will not tolerate violence in our school. We will make every effort to prevent incidents of violence from occurring by adopting, implementing, and enforcing a Violence Prevention Program. We will provide adequate budgetary and implementation resources to ensure that this policy is enforced.

- All staff members of (School Name) are responsible for implementing and maintaining our Violence prevention Program. Our program requires that all employees adhere to work practices that are designed to make the property secure, and to engage in no verbal threats or physical actions that create a hazard to persons on the property. At the same time, students and visitors are expected to conduct themselves in the same manner.
- Any/all acts of violence are to be reported immediately to (designated person[s]) An Incident Report Form shall be completed as soon as any necessary emergency care or related response has been completed.
- Each act of violence reported on an Incident Report Form shall be evaluated by a Threat Assessment Team appointed by (Senior School Administrator). The team shall make appropriate recommendations for remedial actions to prevent another occurrence. School administration shall implement necessary practices.
- All employees and students are responsible for following safe practices, adhering to all directives, policies, procedures and written instructions to maintain a safe, hazard free environment. Any employee or student who disregards such regulations will be disciplined under the (School Name/Authority) discipline policy.
- (School Name) administration is responsible for ensuring that all safety and health and related policies are kept current, and are clearly communicated to all employees and students. Further the administration is responsible for prompt response to reports or recommendations for improvements in site security. The Violence Prevention Program shall be reviewed and updated annually.

Glossary of Terms

Administrative Agencies Established by law for enforcement of specific laws. *Example*: The Equal Employment Opportunity Commission.

Adolescence The developmental period of youth between puberty and completion of physical growth.

Anti-Bullying Legislation Laws passed by many states in varying stringent degrees, but all touching upon the duty of the school district to protect its students against acts of violence or harassment.

Appellate Court A level of court that deals only with *Criminal Cases*.

Assault An act that puts another person in reasonable fear of their bodily harm.

Attention Deficit Disorder ADD) A persistent pattern of inattention and/or hyperactivity-impulsivity that is more frequently displayed and more severe than is typically observed in individuals of comparable levels of development.

Autism A developmental disorder that is characterized by qualitative impairment in social interaction, use of verbal language in communication, and/or use of symbolic-imaginative play.

Battery An unlawful act of physical touching.

BBP Exposure Control Plan A legal (federal and/or state) mandated, written employee protection plan that employers must develop and maintain to ensure that BBP hazards are identified, and appropriate facilities, equipment, and employee training and medical support are in place for employees with exposure to such hazards.

Bloodborne Pathogens (BBP) Pathogenic microorganisms that are present in human blood and can cause diseases in humans. These pathogens include but are not limited to, hepatitis B (HBV), and human immunodeficiency virus (HIV).

Brief A written summary of arguments presented by a lawyer in a court case.

Bullying Any speech, act, or expression intended to intimidate or injure another.

Cerebral Palsy Disorders of the nervous system characteristic by impaired neuromuscular coordination and resulting from damage to the nervous system that occurs during the pre-natal, natal or early post-natal periods of development.

Civil Law Rules which if broken, the violators are punished by monetary penalties (*Damages*) and court orders to comply with the law in the future (*Injunctions*). These are usually enforced through court orders.

Common Law Laws created by courts, often when no statute covers the area. Known as *Common Law* or *Judge Made Law*.

Court Decisions A ruling by a court (usually in the form of a written order) which determines one or more legal issues in a lawsuit or other proceeding before the court.

Court of Appeals (See Intermediate Appellate Court).

Constitutions A type of statute some sort of legislative body usually creates. They deal with the Fundamental Rights of citizens, the structure of government, and the electoral process.

They are more difficult to amend or repeal then a normal statute.

Corporal Punishment A form of student physical discipline, now outlawed in most states. It should be used only when necessary to maintain order, and less severe forms of punishment have proven to be inadequate.

Criminal Law Rules which if broken, sends the wrongdoer to imprisonment, plus having to pay monetary penalties *(fines)*.

Damages (See Civil Law).

Danger Creation Doctrine Where the school district, through its officials, willfully disregarded the risk of a foreseeable injury. This doctrine also involves the district using its authority (or failing to use its authority) resulting in the creation of an opportunity for the injurious act to occur.

Defendant The person or entity being sued by a Plaintiff.

Defense of Another Your right to use whatever force necessary if you have reasonable fear someone is about to do harm to another person (See also *Self-Defense*).

Department of Homeland Security (DHS) A federal agency whose primary purpose is to help prevent, protect against, and respond to acts of terrorism on United States soil.

DOL/OSHA Standard(s) *"Standard"* means a standard which requires conditions, or the adoption or use of one or more practices, means, methods, operations, or processes reasonably necessary or appropriate to provide safe or healthful employment and places of employment.

Duty An obligation to act or to refrain from acting, the violation of which could subject you to liability.

Duty to Retreat Recognized in many states, it is the duty to attempt to remove yourself from danger before resorting to self-defense.

Employer A person or entity having employees.

Equal Employment Opportunity Commission Created by Congress to enforce the *1964 Civil Rights Act* (See *Administrative Agencies*).

Emotional and Behavioral Problem Children A group of children whose difficulties often reflect a complex mix of genetic, environmental and learning factors. These students can be belligerent, irritable, hostile, argumentative and aggressive. Other traits may include emotionally withdrawn, anxious, passive, non-communicative, self-centered, manipulative and emotionally distant.

Exposure Incident A specific eye, mouth, or other mucous membrane non-intact skin or parenteral contact with blood or other potentially infectious materials that results from the performance of the employee's duties. (*Parenteral* means piercing mucous membranes or the skin barrier through such events as needlesticks, human bites, cuts and abrasions).

False Imprisonment An unjustifiable confinement of another person, either literally or through threats of harm to them or others.

Fines A monetary penalty for the breaking the law (See *Criminal Law*).

Gifted Children Exceptional children who learn at accelerated rates and have unique learning styles.

Government Printing Office (GPO) Established by Congress in 1813, it is the Federal Government's primary, centralized resource for gathering, cataloging, producing, providing, authenticating and preserving published information in all its forms.

Gun Free School Act of 1994 This federal law, repealed in 2002, required expulsion of any student found with a weapon on school grounds.

Holmes, Oliver Wendell A famous 19th Century legal scholar, judge, sage and attorney.

Human Immunodeficiency Virus (HIV) A retrovirus that causes Acquired Immunodeficiency Syndrome (**AIDS**). This condition, in turn causes the human body's immune system to fail, which means that the body can no longer defend itself against a wide range of infectious diseases.

Injunctions (See *Civil Law*)

Intentional Torts Includes assault, battery, causing another person severe emotional distress, conversion (taking another person's property), slander, libel or false imprisonment. The key element: *The actor **intended** to commit the act in question.* (See also *Tort*).

In loco parentis The legal obligation in some states that places school officials *"in the place of the child's parents"*.

Intermediate Appellate Court Also called *Court of Appeals*. Hears cases appealed by the losing party at the *Trial Court* level. (See also *Trial Court*).

Judge Made Law (See *Common Law).*

Law A rule or set of rules that govern our behavior and actions.

Learning Disabled Children Normal in physical, cognitive and social development, with specific cognitive difficulties that cause them to learn in unique, unconventional ways.

Limitation on Liability for Teachers – Section 6736 A central provision of the *No Child Left Behind Act of 2001.*

National Institute for Occupational Safety & Health (NIOSH) A division of the Center for Disease Control (CDC), NIOSH is the main U.S. federal agency responsible for conducting research into occupational safety and health matters as well as making recommendations for prevention and control of occupational injuries and illnesses.

Negligence-based Torts Civil wrongs which are not intentional but caused by a breach of the duty to exercise due care.

Negligent Act An act of omission which violates the duty to exercise due care.

No Child Left Behind Act of 2001 A federal law bearing many complicated provisions, most of them containing requirements school districts must comply with to receive federal funding.

Ordinances Enactments of a municipal body such as a city council.

Parenteral Piercing mucous membranes or the skin barrier through such events as needle sticks, human bites, cuts or abrasions.

Personal Protective Equipment (PPE) Specialized clothing or equipment worn by an employee or anyone seeking protection against a hazard.

Piaget, Jean One of the most significant psychologists of the twentieth century. He pioneered *Genetic Epistemology,* the study of the development of knowledge.

Plaintiff The person or entity initiating a lawsuit, thus bearing the burden of proof against the *Defendant.*

Pre-operational Period (Toddler – Preschool) The developmental period ranging from two to six-seven years of age.

Proximate Cause The event or act which directly causes harm.

Punitive Damages Damages awarded to punish or make an example of someone whose conduct is deemed to be outrageous, wanton or reckless (See also *No Child Left Behind*).

Racketeering Influenced and Corrupt Organizations Act (RICO) A federal law designed to punish those who engage in conspiratorial criminal enterprises. Mainly designed to combat organized crime, but has been used in other settings.

Regulated Waste Liquid (or semi-liquid) blood or other potentially infectious materials; contaminated items that would release blood or other potentially infectious materials in a liquid or semi-liquid state if compressed; items caked with dried blood or other potentially infectious materials and capable of releasing these materials during handling; contaminated sharps and pathological and microbial wastes containing blood or other infectious materials.

Regulations Created by an Administrative Agency. Not strictly "*law*", but often having the force of law.

Retardation, Mental Significantly sub-average intellectual and adaptive functioning that is present prior to age eighteen. Areas of delay include communication, self-care, home living, social/interpersonal skills, use of community resources, self-direction, academic skills, work, leisure, health and safety.

Section 1983 a federal law passed shortly after the Civil War prohibiting governmental entities (such as a school district) from depriving individuals of their constitutional rights.

Self-Defense The right to use whatever force is reasonably necessary to protect yourself from harm. (See also *Defense of Another*).

Sensorimotor Period The developmental period from birth to two years of age.

Sharps Infected needles, broken glass products, test tubes.

Special Relationship Doctrine A state's extensive control over a citizen's life obligates it to a heightened duty to protect that citizen. (See also *Section 1983*).

Special Danger (See *Section 1983*)

State Includes a State of the United States, the District of Columbia, Puerto Rico, the Virgin Islands, American Samoa, Guam and the Trust Territory of the Pacific Islands.

State Supreme Court The final (and usually last) appeal level for a decision that was handed down by the *Intermediate Appellate Court*.

Supreme Court The highest federal court in the United States. It consists of nine justices and hears appeals from all federal courts, and also from State Supreme Courts.

Statutes Law executed by a legislative body (could be the U.S. Congress or a state legislature). Also commonly referred to as *Ordinances*.

Supremacy Clause Found in the U.S. Constitution. Federal Law always placed at the top of the pecking order in deciding Federal vs. State law conflicts.

Teeth of the Law Penalties imposed for violating a law.

Tort A civil wrong done to another person; for which the law will provide a remedy. These are either *Intentional Torts* or *Negligence-based Torts*.

Trial Court The lowest court in the Judicial Court System pecking order.

Unconstitutional If a law conflicts with the Constitution, the courts will favor the Constitution.

United States District Court The lowest court in the Federal system having jurisdiction over cases in a geographic area (*District*).

Universal Precautions An approach to infection control that stipulates that all exposures to human blood and certain body fluids must be treated as if known to be infectious for HIV, HBV, and other Bloodborne Pathogens.

Williams-Steiger Occupational Safety and Health Act (OSHA) of 1970 (Effective April 28, 1971). Its intention: *"Assure so far as possible every working man and woman in the nation safe and healthful working conditions, and to preserve our human resources."*

Worker's Compensation A theory of law that provides that the employer is responsible for payment of all medical charges and disability compensation to the injured or ill employee if the injury or illness arose because of conditions in the employer's workplace. In exchange, such charges are limited to amounts specified by statute. In other words, the employee is guaranteed appropriate treatment and continued compensation subject to pre-set limits, and the employer is shielded from unlimited liability. Generally, each state has unique worker's compensation statutes. Certain specific labor classifications or groups are covered by federal programs such as longshoremen and harbor workers, railroad employees and other specific workers.

Zero Tolerance Policies Usually requires immediate suspension or expulsion of a student who possesses a dangerous weapon on school premises. Usually these policies are the result of legislation at the state level.